TOM DALEY

MY STORY

MICHAEL JOSEPH

Published by the Penguin Group

Penguin Books Ltd
80 Strand,
London WC2R 0RL, England

Penguin Group (USA) Inc.
375 Hudson Street,
New York, New York 10014, USA

Penguin Group (Canada)
90 Eglinton Avenue East, Suite 700,
Toronto, Ontario, Canada M4P 2Y3
(a division of Pearson Penguin Canada Inc.)

Penguin Ireland
25 St Stephen's Green,
Dublin 2, Ireland
(a division of Penguin Books Ltd)

Penguin Group (Australia)
250 Camberwell Road,
Camberwell, Victoria 3124, Australia
(a division of Pearson Australia Group Pty Ltd)

Penguin Books India Pvt Ltd
11 Community Centre,
Panchsheel Park, New Delhi – 110 017, India

Penguin Group (NZ)
67 Apollo Drive, Rosedale, Auckland 0632,
New Zealand
(a division of Pearson New Zealand Ltd)

Penguin Books (South Africa) (Pty) Ltd
Block D, Rosebank Office Park
181 Jan Smuts Avenue, Parktown North,
Gauteng 2193 South Africa

Penguin Books Ltd, Registered Offices:
80 Strand, London WC2R 0RL, England

www.penguin.com

First published 2012
1

Printed in Germany by Mohn Media

Colour reproduction by Altaimage Ltd

A CIP catalogue record for this book is available
from the British Library

Set in Swiss

ISBN: 978–0–718–15807–1

www.greenpenguin.co.uk

MIX
Paper from
responsible sources
FSC™ C018179

Penguin Books is committed to a sustainable
future for our business, our readers and our planet.
This book is made from Forest Stewardship
Council™ certified paper.

ALWAYS LEARNING   **PEARSON**

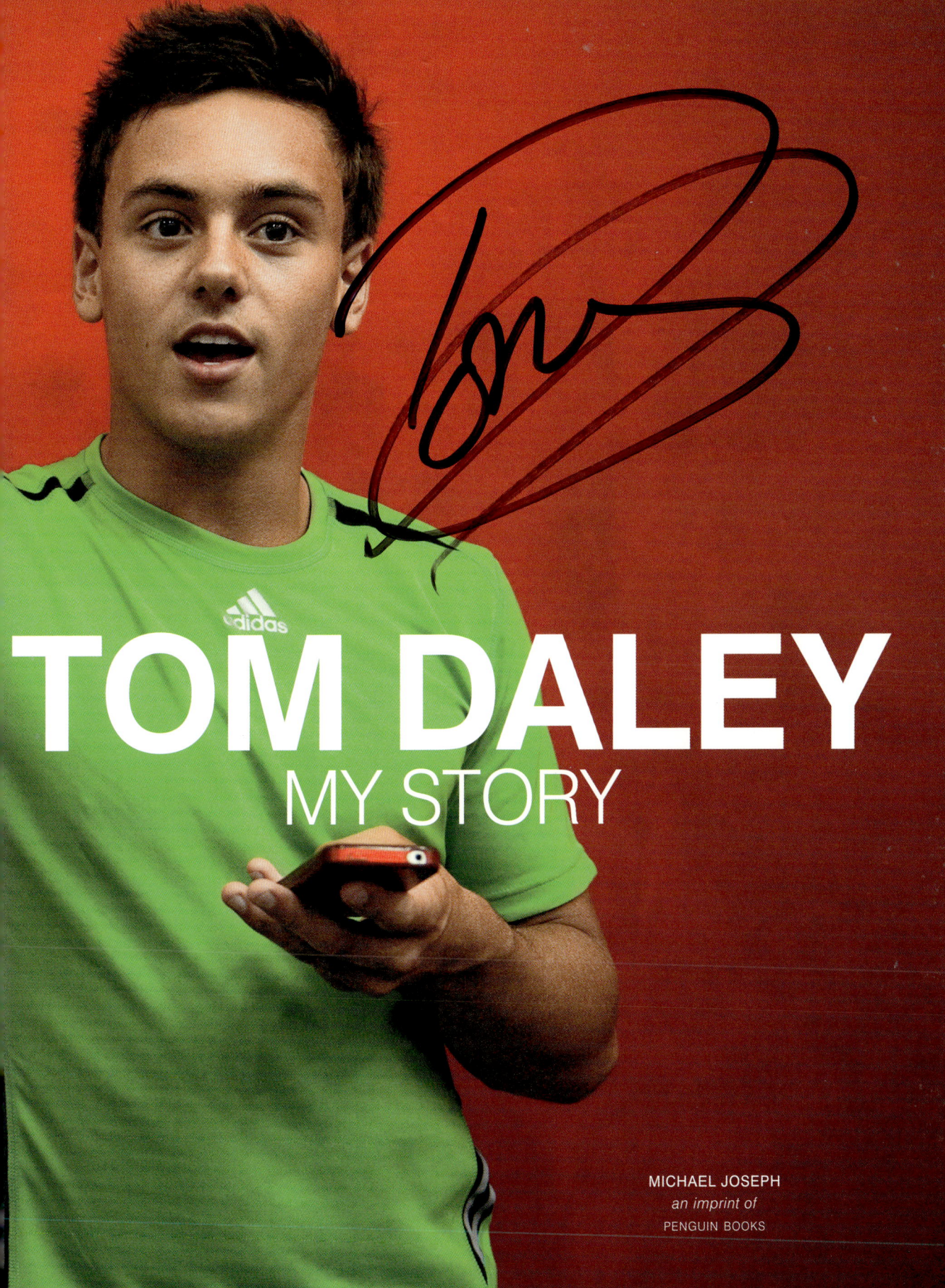

TOM DALEY

MY STORY

MICHAEL JOSEPH

an imprint of

PENGUIN BOOKS

'Courage is the thing.
All goes if courage goes.'

J. M. Barrie, the author of *Peter Pan*

CONTENTS

PROLOGUE

Standing on top of the 10m board I have butterflies and feel a rush of adrenalin. No matter how many times I've dived from this platform, it scares me. It's like taking a leap into the unknown because every dive is different.

The 10m platform at the pool in Plymouth where I train every day is considered one of the hardest boards to dive off in the world. The domed, concrete ceiling is low, so it feels like it is caving in on you, and the board is almost half the size of ordinary 10m platforms and wobbles when you stand on it.

Looking out, I can see miniature people doing front crawl up and down the regular pool, women bobbing up and down at aqua-aerobics or mothers making their way to a baby session with their youngsters in tow. A dozen sunken hair-bands sit lifeless on the bottom of the pool beneath me, along with a white, human-sized dummy, for the life-saving classes. I am immune to the sweet and sticky smell of chlorine; to me, the pool smells as familiar as home.

There are always echoing noises – children laughing, music playing and people talking, but when I stand up there, I am in my own bubble of silence. There is so much space around me it's almost like I am standing on a concrete block that is suspended in mid-air.

By the time I have reached the top, via a chain of worn wooden ladders, I have already visualized the dive in my head a number of times. I go through every movement in my mind and the way my body will coil, tuck, whirl and twist, like elastic. I don't think about the landing, I concentrate on the process. I am totally focused. I dry myself with my soft chamois cloth so my hands do not slip when I bend into a tuck or pike position. It's also very, very hot and clammy and moisture starts to seep back into your skin so you have to wipe it away. Before I start a training session or competition, I also rub Palmolive soap on my arms and legs because it helps me grip. If you slip out of a dive, it's a disaster.

I try to breathe slowly and steadily and not think too hard about what I'm about to do. If you think too much the demons start crawling into your head and you imagine all the things that could go wrong: What if I land badly? What if I lose myself in the air? What if I miss my hands? I have to focus on each step at a time.

The hardest dive on my list is the front four and a half somersaults with tuck – sometimes called 'The Big Front' – and it is so technically and physically challenging that people in the sport once thought it was impossible. But with a difficulty rating of 3.7, it will be key to me doing well at the Olympics. It's a make-or-break dive: do it well and the competition could be yours, perform it badly and you may end up throwing a medal away.

I think about 2012 every day, and often I look at the clock when it says 20.12 – it feels symbolic in some way. Recently I was filming an advert and it was on the twelfth take that it was perfect. It's really freaky. Every day when I train, I wonder what it will be like, standing on the top board at the London Aquatics Centre. It's good to imagine how it will be because it puts added pressure on me and gets the adrenalin pumping around my body.

For 'The Big Front', I take a run-up from the back of the board. I make sure my shoulders are relaxed, so I don't look anxious, but every other muscle is tense and feels solid and strong. I count myself in, to urge myself to run, saying aloud, 'One, two, three…', take a deep breath and go. I run on my toes – it's almost like a hop, skip and a jump – four steps to give me power and momentum as I take off and launch myself into the air.

Immediately I snap into a tuck, clutching my knees to my chest. I don't know how I do it, it's like my brain just knows. There are memory patterns in the brain called 'schemas' – these are the movement patterns that are ingrained into your mind through hours and hours of repetitive practice on dry land and in the pool. I get into the correct shape at the right time and make decisions in split seconds. It's like I have an internal compass – I know where my body is at any time when I am in the air, which direction it needs to go or if I need to slow my rotation or speed it up. A tiny movement can make a dive, or completely ruin it.

As I spin round, it feels like I am going in slow motion and on some occasions, it even feels like I have lots of time. I have to use my eyes. If I close them I could land flat on the water. The force is so hard, it's like a car crash. You bruise immediately, and can split skin open or cough up blood.

I have to see every single detail – or 'spot' – even though I am falling at up to 34 miles per hour. You get used to feeling queasy, like you're whirling on a rollercoaster. I look for the pool water, which is a snatch of bright blue. I count it five times so quickly I don't even register that I am doing it and at the very last millisecond, at the height of the 3m board, I stretch out as far and as sharply and as hard as I can, reaching for the water with my strongest hand – my left hand first, then clasp my right hand on top. Every muscle from my hands, through my arms, torso and legs to my pointed toes is squeezed tight so when I punch the water it does not hurt. It helps that I have big hands, which give me a larger surface area on entry, lessening the crashing impact. It takes 1.9 seconds from takeoff and, after dropping the height of two double decker buses, I hit the water at over 34 miles per hour.

I can tell if I've done a good dive because as I strike the water and split my hands apart it creates a vacuum, so I immediately get sucked under – in a 'rip' entry – and water pulls me down, perfectly straight, like an arrow. The immediate feeling is a sense of relief that I haven't hurt myself. If I'm at a competition and I've done a good dive, I race as fast as I can towards the surface of the water through the muffled cheers and whistles. I can't wait to see the electronic board with the name 'Thomas Daley' in shiny neon letters, next to a row of high scores, and to look up to see my family cheering and the GB team on their feet, clapping and hollering words of encouragement.

I strive every time for a complete set of perfect 10s. When the points are high or I know I've won a medal, I feel I have so much energy I could leap out of the water like a dolphin.

As I climb out of the water, picking up my chamois cloth on the way, I always think about Dad. He was at almost every training session and competition that I did, until he died in May 2011, and every time I train I expect to see him sitting by the poolside, grinning and cracking jokes, making everyone around him laugh.

HE WAS NOT ONLY MY DAD; HE WAS MY BEST FRIEND, SOUNDING BOARD, TAXI DRIVER AND BIGGEST CHAMPION. WHEN I JUMP FROM THE BOARD AT LONDON 2012, IT WILL BE FOR HIM.

DIVING IN

'I LOVE THE FEELING OF WEIGHTLESSNESS.
I ALWAYS LOVE BEING IN THE WATER AND TO
COMBINE JUMPING OFF THE SIDE INTO THE WATER
FEELS LIKE A DIFFERENT AND FUN WAY TO BE ABLE
TO SWIM. I FEEL FREE, LIKE I COULD DO ANYTHING.'

Just moments after I was born, the midwife dunked me in a bath of water and I made this funny 'oooooohhhh' noise through pursed lips.

'THIS ONE'S A WATER BABY,' SHE EXCLAIMED. 'AND LOOK AT HIS BIG HANDS!' LITTLE DID SHE KNOW THAT THOSE TWO ATTRIBUTES WOULD HELP DEFINE MY LIFE SO FAR.

It was 21 May 1994 and I was one of the first babies to make an entrance at the newly opened maternity ward at Derriford hospital in Plymouth. I was my mum and dad's first baby and they were young parents aged twenty-three and twenty-four.

I was an easy-going and bright baby with a keen sense of adventure. My first December I gave everyone a scare when I crawled at top speed over to the newly decorated Christmas tree and pulled it over on top of myself. Like most babies, I never wanted to go to sleep – and everyone used to sing Pato Banton's 'Baby Come Back' to me, which apparently had the desired effect of making me drop off into a deep slumber.

I loved drawing, jigsaws and colouring in and was a total perfectionist – if it wasn't just how I wanted it, I would cry. I started talking very early, was walking at ten months and by eighteen months I could write my own name. I was obsessed with Big Bird from Sesame Street and Snow White and the Seven Dwarfs – or 'dig digs' as I called them, after the song.

When I was two, my brother William was born and I loved him instantly. I was very affectionate and not long after he was brought home from hospital, I climbed into his carrycot to give him a cuddle – not realizing that I almost squashed and suffocated him. Sorry, Will!

Both my parents, Debbie and Rob, were
born and grew up in Plymouth. They had
been together since they were fifteen and got
married when they were both twenty-one. I
am surrounded by family: my dad's parents
Grandma Rose and Granddad Dave, who
we call Granddad Dink, and my Aunty Marie,
Dad's sister, who was fifteen when I was born,
used to live a few doors up on the road where
we lived in Derriford. As soon as I could walk I
sometimes let myself out the garden gate and
toddled up to their house, sending my mum
into a panic, until she realized where I was.

Mum's parents Grandma Jenny and Granddad
Doug, Dad's brother Uncle Jamie, and his
wife Aunty Debbie and my Aunty Marie, who is

TOP LEFT
The Daley Gang . . .

TOP MIDDLE
*Fun in the water
with Dad.*

TOP RIGHT
*Me striking a pose,
Will looking cute for
once and Ben looking
starstruck.*

now married to Uncle Jason, and loads of cousins are also in Plymouth. There are always people popping in and out of the house. My mum's two brothers – Kevin and Brian – and their families live in London.

I come from a family of hard workers; both Mum and Dad left school at sixteen and went straight into jobs, Dad worked for a company that built special-purpose machinery, a business that he would later run, while Mum worked as a receptionist and later for Toshiba. Granddad Dink was a toolmaker and Granddad Doug a builder.

Plymouth is a large seaside city on the south-west coast. The city centre is fairly modern, having been rebuilt from the 1940s after being bombed out in the war. It's the place to be in the summer! It is a great place to grow up, with Dartmoor on one side, Cornwall on the other and the Hoe just a few miles away; much of my early childhood was spent outdoors. We often went camping and as a toddler I loved feeding the ducks at Tavistock Park and going on long walks.

When I was three, my favourite meals were chicken nuggets and spaghetti on toast but my love affair with food reached new heights when I got into baking with my Aunty Marie. We loved making cupcakes together, mixing the batter and licking the spoons, before decorating the new batch with icing and sweets.

Mum and Dad were keen for me to be able to handle myself in the water because we lived by the sea, so I started swimming regularly at the pool at Fort Stamford, near my Grandma Rose and Granddad Dink's house, when I was a toddler. As soon as I was confident in the water, I went on a week-long intensive course for half an hour a day and picked up my five-metre certificate.

When I was three, we moved to the house I live in now in Eggbuckland, perched on the top of a hill with amazing, panoramic views over the local area, which is made up of mostly post-war, cream-coloured homes. Plymouth is milder and wetter than the rest of the country, so it is often grey and raining. Seagulls provide the constant background soundtrack.

Ten days before my fifth birthday my youngest brother, Ben, was born. I was equally besotted with him and we shared a room until I was almost sixteen, when we had an extension above the kitchen built so I could have my own space and Ben wasn't disturbed when I came home late from training.

On my first day at my local primary school, St Edward's, there were no tears – I enjoyed every second. I did normal schoolwork and enjoyed sports like judo, squash and tennis. I was also terrible at lots of other sports; Mum took me to football lessons and I was awful. I could not

TOP

*Trophy time – my
favourite throw was a
'Tomoe nage' because
it had my name in it.*

catch a ball either, and when I tried to kick it, it
would just go in the opposite direction.

I was also a fan of a soft-play area called Jump
nearby, where I clambered into ballpits, threw
myself down slides and crawled up huge
climbing frames. I was naturally athletic and
during one wedding that all the family was at I
shocked the other guests when I walked from
one side of the dancefloor to the other on
my hands.

We were definitely a household of boys; Granddad Dink had a speedboat and Dad had a jet-ski which we used to ride on and I loved the exhilarating feeling of speeding along in the water as the salt spray blew around us. Our days out fell into a familiar routine with Mum organizing us all with spare clothes, any kit we needed, food and drink and making sure we made it on time, while Dad packed the car with all the 'fun' stuff. He was always joking and mostly acted like a big kid, while Mum battled to keep us all in line!

In our summer holidays before I started diving, we would go to the South of France with our family in a trailer tent, sometimes for three weeks at a time. Mum, Dad, William, Ben and I and my Uncle Steve and Aunty Kerry – Steve is Dad's cousin – and their two children, Joe and Sam, would take the ferry from Plymouth across the Channel to Roscoff and motor down through France to stay on a caravan site. I remember being outdoors from morning until we went to bed, learning to ride a bike there, playing endless games of rounders, splashing about in the pool and Sam over-stretching our Stretch Armstrong gel-filled toy and all the green goo coming out. The ultimate highlight was our electric car, which we used to drive around the site. Sam and I were the eldest, so we were in the front, with one of us steering and one accelerating, and William and Joe would sit in the back. We used to think we were so cool – but it only went at 4 mph!

One day when I was seven we decided to go for a family day out at the Central Park Pool, which is about ten minutes from our house. They were putting on a fun session with giant, colourful inflatables, where you can go down slides and hang off mats.

As I ran out of the changing room, in front of me was the main pool, which was so big it felt like a giant arena. I was bowled over.

Music was playing in the background and people were laughing and talking by the poolside. It felt so exciting.

Next to the main area was a diving pool. People were jumping off the high 5m and 7m platforms and the 3m and 1m springboards.

BUT IT WAS THE 10M PLATFORM THAT REALLY GOT MY EYES POPPING OUT OF MY HEAD. IT WAS SO HIGH UP AND I HELD MY BREATH EVERY TIME SOMEONE WALKED TO THE EDGE OF THE BOARD AND JUMPED. I WAS CAPTIVATED.

Dad's attack with lemon juice had an effect on my hair – it wasn't highlights, I promise!

I didn't even want to swim and Dad had to virtually drag me away.

'That looks like fun, can I learn?' I asked Mum.

We picked up a leaflet and my parents booked William and me in for five lessons, starting the following weekend. Dad used to joke that it was the best £25 he ever spent.

On the day of my first lesson one Saturday morning, I left the changing room and walked out towards the diving pool, but at the entrance there was a 'Pool Closed' sign. I legged it back to the changing room and sat on one of the benches, deflated. I felt so disappointed. Dad reassured me that it was just because I was so early and when I went back out, thankfully someone saw me looking upset and opened the gate. As I entered the poolside, I looked up

and saw Dad waving down at me from the balcony and giving me a huge grin and a big thumbs-up. He barely missed a single session after that.

In our first lesson, we jumped off the side of the pool and off the 1m springboard. I love the feeling of weightlessness. I always love being in the water and to combine jumping off the side into the water feels like a different and fun way to be able to swim. I felt free, like I could do anything.

William was a better diver than me. However hard I tried to pick up the dives immediately, he always seemed to get them quicker. Like most brothers, I loved the fun sense of competition between us. There were other kids there too, but from the beginning we were always chasing each other.

ABOVE

The family caravan. My dad would say, 'Don't come knocking when the caravan is rocking!'

RIGHT

Me as Elvis!

Not long after we started diving, Mum and Dad bought a caravan and we used to motor across to Watergate Bay in Newquay most weekends. We spent our days on our bikes, swimming, playing cricket or tennis, or at the clubhouse where they had kids' clubs running every day to keep us all entertained. I loved karaoke and Dad told me that he thought singing in front of an audience would help with the nerves when I was diving, so we would go to the clubhouse and I would belt out S Club 7's 'Reach for the Stars'. It obviously worked, because at my Aunty Marie's wedding I dressed up as Elvis in a mini white and gold jumpsuit and sang one of his classics, 'Don't be Cruel'.

Around then I was watching *Blue Peter* when they said they were looking for people to audition for this new band, S Club Juniors, based on the adult version, only for kids. I made Dad video my audition on a camcorder in the front room. It was really funny. I was getting really stressed out because I could not hear the music but Dad kept telling me that they needed to hear my voice. In the end, the video was of me singing, while also listening to the music through my earphones and doing an accompanying dance. I waited for a letter telling me I had the job but I never heard back from anyone. I hope the BBC never dig up that tape!

In December 2001 I got my first diving certificate, called Preliminary, for doing various dives off poolside, including forward and back dives, and floating in the tuck position in the pool. Forward dives always felt quite natural, but when I started to learn back dives for the first time, my instinct was to keep looking over my shoulder. It felt strange not being able to see where I was going; it's like diving blind. The same day I got my Level 1 award for another list of moves like jumping off the side without swinging my arms and a forward tuck roll in the water.

I would look forward to every Saturday morning, when I would eagerly rush out of the changing rooms straight to the diving area to learn something new and, as the year progressed, I worked my way through the levels, which gradually introduced different, more complicated moves. Each time I got a colourful certificate to add to my collection, Dad would take it and laminate it in a special file he had created to keep everything together.

During the summer of 2002, the Commonwealth Games were on the TV. I was eight years old. My family and I watched the competition from our front room and I made sure we were recording it too. There would always be a race for the remote – if William or Ben got hold of it, I would never stand a chance.

I became obsessed and watched the videos of the British divers Pete Waterfield and Leon Taylor and the Canadian diver Alexandre Despatie diving over and over and over again, until Mum and Dad got really annoyed that they could not watch their programmes. I was fascinated by the way they somersaulted through the air so seamlessly. It was as if it didn't take any effort at all to jump off the platform, spin around and hit the water with barely a splash. I kept thinking that I wanted to be able to do that and to execute the dives that they were doing. I learnt that Alex had won the 1998 Commonwealth Games gold medal on the 10m platform when he was just thirteen. He was my new hero.

Throughout the competition, the commentators kept mentioning the Olympics. I had never heard of them and asked Dad what they were.

'It's the biggest sporting event on the planet,' he told me.
'It's the biggest competition you could ever do.'
'Ah right,' I said, mulling it over. 'Wow. That sounds amazing.'

'The next one is in Athens in 2004, then it's in Beijing in 2008,' Dad said. 'There is some talk that London will bid again to host the event in 2012.'

I went upstairs and started researching it on the Internet. We had a computer on the landing that we all used to share and I found a picture of the flag. Dad came upstairs and sat by me, explaining that every country in the world had at least one colour from the Olympic rings in it and that the interlocking circles signified the continents coming together. I looked at all the different sports that there were from countries I had never even heard of.

I drew a picture. In between two sets of blue, yellow, black, green and red rings is a sausage man in a pair of Union Jack Speedos with spiky hair and big eyes doing a handstand at the Olympics in London 2012. Above are the words 'My Ambition' in bubble writing. It was my dream then, and still is now, to perform the best dives of my life there – to dive out of my socks.

I drew the picture imagining myself standing on the rostrum in London with my gold medal heavy around my neck.

MASTERING
THE BASICS

My first competition was in March 2003. William had dropped out by then, because he was bored and wanted to concentrate on football and rugby at the weekends instead. Everyone in the diving club at the Central Park Pool was invited and the spectator area was filled with parents clapping and cheering on their kids. After doing a forward dive off poolside and a tuck dive off the 1m springboard, I was given a small silver trophy. All I could think was, 'Oh my god! I've been given a trophy,' and I wanted to do the competition again. I put it in pride of place on the shelf in my bedroom.

After my win, I was put into the competitive squad. Our group was called the Weenies because we were the most junior divers and my coach was a woman called Sam Grevett. She was the scary one that everyone was terrified of. Andy Banks, who trains me now, was the other Head Coach and he and Sam ran the business together. We were still only training once a week but Sam taught me the basics of good technique and about discipline and attention to detail. She showed me how important it is to master the basic dive before you move on to the harder version.

We learnt about the fundamentals of competitions. Springboard dives are arranged into five groups: forward, where the diver faces forwards and rotates forwards; back, where the diver faces backwards and rotates backwards; reverse group, where the diver faces forwards and rotates backwards towards the board; inward, where the diver faces backwards and rotates forwards towards the board; and twist, where the diver performs a dive from any of the above group, but at the same time, they twist their body about a longitudinal axis. The sixth group, added for the platform competition, is the armstand group, where the diver is on their hands facing the board with their back to the water and rotates over to somersault forwards, or cuts

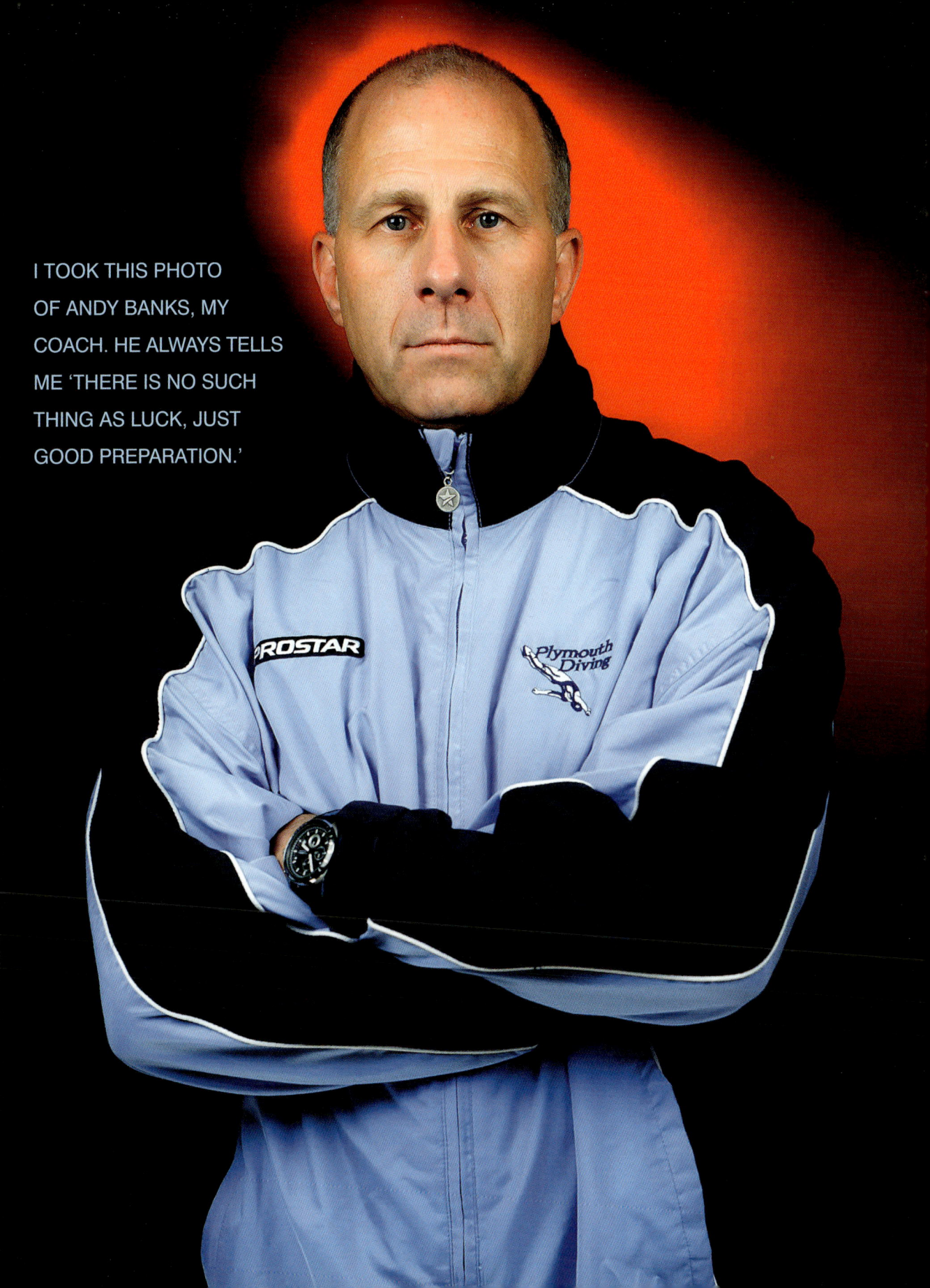

I TOOK THIS PHOTO
OF ANDY BANKS, MY
COACH. HE ALWAYS TELLS
ME 'THERE IS NO SUCH
THING AS LUCK, JUST
GOOD PREPARATION.'

through their hands to
rotate in a reverse direction
Alternatively, a diver can be on
their hands facing the water with their back
to the board and rotating backwards.

Most dives in these groups can be performed
in any one of three positions: straight, where the
body and legs are straight with no bending at the
hips or knees; piked, with the body bent at hips,
legs straight without bending at the knees; and
tucked, when the body is bunched up close to the
knees, bent at the hips and knees, with elbows in,
hands clasping the shins.

Competitions are conducted by a referee, five
judges, two recorders, a computer operator
and an announcer. After each dive, the referee
signals to the judges, who input their scores
into the computer pad or flash scorecards.
The points scored can range from 0 to 10.
The judge will consider the approach or
starting position, takeoff, flight and entry of
the dive, and then post an award having

looked at the dive as a whole. Judges do not take the difficulty of the dive into consideration.

The recorders copy down the judges' scores and deduct the highest and lowest mark. They then multiply the remaining three awards by the tariff (degree of difficulty) of the dive.

EACH DIVE IS AFFORDED A TARIFF. THIS RANGES FROM 1.2 UP TO 4.7 FOR THE MORE COMPLICATED DIVES. THIS MEANS THAT THE DIVER WHO CAN COMPETENTLY PERFORM HIGHER-TARIFF DIVES CAN OFTEN HAVE THE ADVANTAGE OVER THE ONE WITH EASIER DIVES. HOWEVER, THIS IS ONLY THE CASE IF THE DIVER PERFORMS THE MORE DIFFICULT DIVE WELL.

For example:

A back dive from 1m has a tariff of 1.5
If the dive scores 5s from all judges = 15 points
15 × 1.5 = 22.50 in total

A reverse dive tucked from 1m has a tariff of 1.6
If the dive scores 5s from all the judges = 15 points
15 × 1.6 = 24.00 in total

However, if the back dive scores 5.5s from all the judges = 16.50 points
16.5 × 1.5 = 24.75 in total

If the reverse dive scores 4.5s from all judges = 13.50 points
13.5 × 1.6 = 21.60 in total

Each dive is also given a number code, so it can be explained quickly. For example, a forward three and a half somersaults in a tuck position (107c) carries a tariff of 2.8.

There are various penalties. The most common are: a failed dive where the amount of rotation or twist is not within 90 degrees of the pre-declared amount and the diver receives no points; the restart – if a diver stops or pauses after starting, or if, when performing an armstand dive, the diver's feet return to touch the board, the diver will restart and have two points deducted from the overall score; if the diver shows a flight position other than the one declared in advance, the judges will be instructed to award no more than two points for the dive. Finally, on entering the water headfirst divers must have their arms positioned beyond their heads so their hands strike the water first, and for foot-first entries they must have their arms held by their sides. Failure to observe these arm positions on entry into the water will result in the referee instructing judges to award no more than four and a half points for the dive.

I also learned that the judges are looking for lots of things: a good, smooth approach; the takeoff needs to show control and balance and a good angle; elevation; a good execution – with a clean technique and form. The most important part is the entry because that's the thing the judges see last so it's normally what they remember. It needs to be near vertical, with the smallest amount of splash possible. However, since judges must give their scores instantaneously, they base their scores more on a gut instinct and overall impression rather than actual calculation.

When we started talking about competitions I got this bubble of excitement in my belly, I could not wait to start. I also started to get nervous, hoping that I could perform the dives I had been doing really well in training sessions at the competitions. Most of all, I could not wait to get more trophies. They would always be sat glistening on the side of the pool and I wanted to fill my shelf at home with as many as I could.

I started doing my certificates off the 1m springboard – from forward jumps to learning special hurdle steps to give you height and spring off the board. I had a real lightning bolt moment when I learnt a forward double somersault from 1m.

After I came out of the water I was so shocked at how easy I found it to perform something that no one else in my group could do. It felt strange that I was routinely landing the right way up when everyone else in the group wasn't able to. I think, for me, it signalled the start of my belief in my ability – it was like a switch had been flicked.

Another day I saw Sam's eyes light up was when I started to learn to twist – a very simple move, just one backward somersault with half a twist, but Sam had been very specific with me about where my arms should be throughout the skill and, on this particular occasion, she stood next to me and asked me to show her where my arms should be and, then, where mine had been. I was able to relay to her exactly where my arms had been throughout different phases of the dive. When my left arm was doing something different to the right arm while my body was somersaulting and twisting, I could show her exactly what my arms had done. She told me that it was a special skill to have an innate internal compass that would enable me to 'feel' where I was during multiple somersaulting and twisting dives. She said that it's not something she can teach and only a tiny few are lucky enough to be born with it. I always knew where I was and could see where I was, meaning that I was already far more consistent than most of my peers.

THE GUT-WRENCHING FEAR OF TRYING NEW DIVES OR HURTING MYSELF, PARTICULARLY WHACKING MY HEAD, WAS ALWAYS THERE. BY THAT POINT, I HAD HIT MY HEAD TWICE.

The first time it was after a swimming lesson and I was doing some dives off the poolside. I jumped and clipped my head on the stone side on the way in. As weird as it sounds, I didn't realize what I had done, and got out to jump in again. It was when I climbed out of the pool for the second time that everything was a blur in front of me. People started walking up to me with concerned looks on their faces, asking if I was OK. I turned round and there was a puddle of crimson red in the pool, like there had been a shark attack. I touched my hand against my forehead and as I took it away I saw the blood. Mum rushed me to hospital but I made such a fuss about having proper stitches because I was so terrified. I didn't want the doctors anywhere near me. In the end they gave me paper ones – or 'origami' as Dad called them – and I still have a scar today. I wish I had had stitches. You can't really see it normally but when I catch the sun it goes a different colour.

A few months after that we were on holiday in Spain and I was messing around in the pool with Dad and my brothers. I was doing backward somersaults off the poolside and there was a shallow ledge before the water dropped down and I cracked the top of my head on the way in because I didn't jump out far enough. That time I knew exactly what I had done; it felt like an iron weight had smashed me around the head. Mum and Dad rushed me in my little brother Ben's pushchair to the Medical Centre nearby, where I had loads of stitches. I remember crying a lot because it was so painful. It didn't deter me though – I loved every second of my diving and my desire to be a good diver would ultimately prove to be greater than my fear.

A month off my ninth birthday, in April 2003, I was entered into the National Novice competition, which Plymouth Diving were hosting. There were thirty divers of my age in my group. There was never any pressure, it was just fun.

Dad kept saying, 'Even if you come last Tom, it means you are thirtieth best in the UK for your age.'

'THIRTIETH BEST IN THE UK! THAT'S AMAZING,' I WOULD THINK, AND NOT WORRY. MUM AND DAD'S ATTITUDE WAS ALWAYS TO DO WHAT YOU LOVED BUT AS SOON AS YOU STOPPED LOVING IT TO STOP. I HAVE ALWAYS HELD THIS PHILOSOPHY BUT AM PASSIONATE ABOUT MY SPORT.

At that time, I never realized I could have a career in diving but, like now, I had good days and bad days. On the rubbish days, when I'm frustrated, I think, 'I've had enough, that's it.' But as soon as I step away, I know I could never give it up. I love it too much.

I came away from the National Novices with a silver medal and 103.80 points for my six dives off the 1m and 3m springboards. I was so chuffed and could not stop smiling.

Afterwards an Australian lady came up to me on the poolside.

'Well done. Can we borrow you for a second?' she asked. I didn't know who she was or what she did at that point. She started measuring how long my legs were compared to my upper body and the length of my arms. She asked me to do a tuck jump and then sit on the floor and do a pike shape to test my flexibility. Then, after I had changed, I did a sprint test to see how quickly I could accelerate over thirty metres.

The lady's name was Chelsea Warr and she ran a National Lottery-funded programme for divers across the country, called World Class Start, in which they coached a group of young people they thought could be capable of achieving international success in diving. She explained that they ran nine weekend training camps a year where they had access to the best coaches and a full team of sports scientists for nutrition, psychology, physiology and physiotherapy.

'I'll be in touch in a couple of months,' she said. 'There's a training camp in Southampton and we'd love you to come along.'

That's when my diving took off. Every Saturday I'd be standing at the door at home hurrying Dad along so we weren't late for training. When I got into the pool, Sam would push me hard. I was very nervous and sometimes stood at the end of the board and refused to dive but she would not let me get away with it.

'You can't be a diver if you don't do this dive. This is one of the dives you need to be able to do,' she would yell after I refused to jump.

I battled with my nerves and often I didn't want to learn new dives, but she kept shouting until I did them. Doing inward dives for the first time was scary because you take off with your back to the water and rotate towards the board, so you have to jump far enough away to be clear of it when you start somersaulting and you can always see it in front of you, which is terrifying. Reverse dives feel equally strange because you rotate backwards and the platform always seems really close to your face.

Some days, after refusing to learn a new dive, I would get out of the pool, shower and change and go out to the car. Then, just as Dad was turning on the ignition, I would regret not doing the dive Sam had asked me to do, feel a bit stupid and would head back to the changing room, put my trunks back on and go back out and do the dive.

One Saturday, during one of my sessions I was meant to be learning a new reverse dive. I didn't know it then but Sam had asked Andy Banks to come and watch me. I stood at the back of the board and refused to jump. I hid behind the 3m pillar, told Sam I didn't want to do it and then promptly burst into tears. The thought of jumping off the board and spinning backwards was horrible.

ANDY TOLD SAM, 'THAT KID WILL NEVER BE A DIVER AS LONG AS HE HAS A HOLE IN HIS ARSE.' I GUESS HE JUST THOUGHT I WAS TOO MUCH OF A WIMP. WE LAUGH ABOUT THAT NOW!

I did eventually do the dive the following week and, rather than feeling scared, it felt great, like I had accomplished something massive. I knew I needed to trust Sam and from there my learning curve went vertical as I started to do more and more dives off the higher platforms.

By July, I was learning dives off the 5m platform, which felt incredibly high. Looking over the edge, the pool seemed so much smaller than it did from 3m. I used this technique where I just made myself jump because once my feet had left the board, I could not get back onto it, even if I wanted to. So I would force myself to leap and would just have to try to do the dive that I was learning while I waited to hit the water. It worked.

Every week, the diving club used to write a newsletter for its members called 'The Jubbly' and after learning the inward one and a half somersaults and inward one and a half piked from 5m, there was a little write-up saying, 'We think he has been taking brave pills recently. Well done, Thomas, keep up the hard work.'

Mum and Dad received a letter about the Southampton training weekend in September with World Class Start. I was so excited to be going off without my parents. I would be sharing a room with one of the other kids and I thought about diving all day, followed by midnight feasts, with sweets on tap – kiddie heaven!

The reality could not have been more different. While we dived during the day and I was constantly happy, as soon as it came to bedtime, I was engulfed with chronic homesickness. I hated it and from then on in was probably known as 'the Hell Child' by all the chaperones. I didn't want to stay in the room, I could not sleep and I just didn't want to be there. I used to say stuff like, 'I'd rather jump out the window than stay here,' while hanging off the windowsill, and, 'I'd rather be dead than be on this training camp.' In the end, they gave into my pleas to ring my parents, who were staying in a nearby hotel after driving me up.

'We'll get a toy from Toys R Us when you come back,' Dad said. Just stick with it. You'll be back home on Sunday.'
'I don't want a toy, I want a monkey,'
'We'll buy it for you tomorrow, if you stay.'
'I don't want to stay,'
'What about a trampoline?'
'I don't want to stay . . . but I do want a monkey and a trampoline.'

I didn't stay in the end because I was so inconsolable. Eventually, a weary Mum and Dad came to pick me up and I slept on the sofa in their hotel room. But, true to their promise, on our return home they bought me a small aerobics trampoline and the cuddly monkey, which has been my lucky charm ever since. I still take it to every competition I go to. He sits in my bag and I zip it up but let his head pop out so he can see where we are going. I fully expect he'll be on poolside for the Olympics.

From a diving perspective, the WCS camps were excellent. We learnt all the basic technical aspects such as entries, somersault programmes, hurdle steps, warm-ups and twisting. As well as the

World Class Start coach Dan Harrison, there was a Chinese director, Cheng Yang, who helped us with our technique. They also tried to make it fun, with talent contests in the evening, where we were scored by the coaches, all-round training like ballet lessons to help us strengthen our muscles, and visits to outdoor pursuits centres, where we would go abseiling and climbing, to help build our confidence.

I was progressing through the groups at Central Park very quickly and soon I was training three times a week with Sam. I also started doing an extra two-hour session of dry-land training, where I did body conditioning, practised moves on a trampoline and developed my skills on the dry board, where you land in a crash mat. The constant impact on your body of diving into water can take its toll, so training on dry land reduces the stress on your joints. It also isolates specific skills so you can practise and perfect each move on its own, before putting it together into a dive. I also worked with small weights to help tone up and strengthen certain body areas.

Later, when a squash court was converted at the Mayflower Centre for us to use as our dry-land training area, I learned new dives in a rig where you are strapped in and can rotate and twist in the air while 'the rigger' allows you to go as fast or slow as you need. You need a certain amount of speed to tip the somersaults and it's good to do them as fast as possible so it is as close to how it is when you are doing the dive in the pool. This kind of work now takes up 60 per cent of my training time, so it was vital to start learning when I was young.

Sam knew what made me tick and could read my mood and she knew when to put pressure on me, and when to leave me alone to just get on with it. Learning new dives made me really chirpy, and the higher up the platforms I got, the more inspired I became.

OFTEN I WAS HESITANT BUT SAM SOON LEARNED, WHEN IT WAS TIME FOR ME TO LEARN A NEW DIVE, NOT TO JUST SPRING IT ON ME AT THE BEGINNING OF A SESSION BECAUSE I HATED THE SURPRISE ELEMENT.

She would give me three days' notice and tell me we would be practising it during our next meeting. I seemed to accept that; I just needed to get my head around it.

I was finding that I was mastering new dives very quickly. I remember one week when I picked up a forward two and a half somersaults with tuck and a back one and a half somersaults with one and a half twists, both from 3m. I could not practise enough; I was totally single-minded.

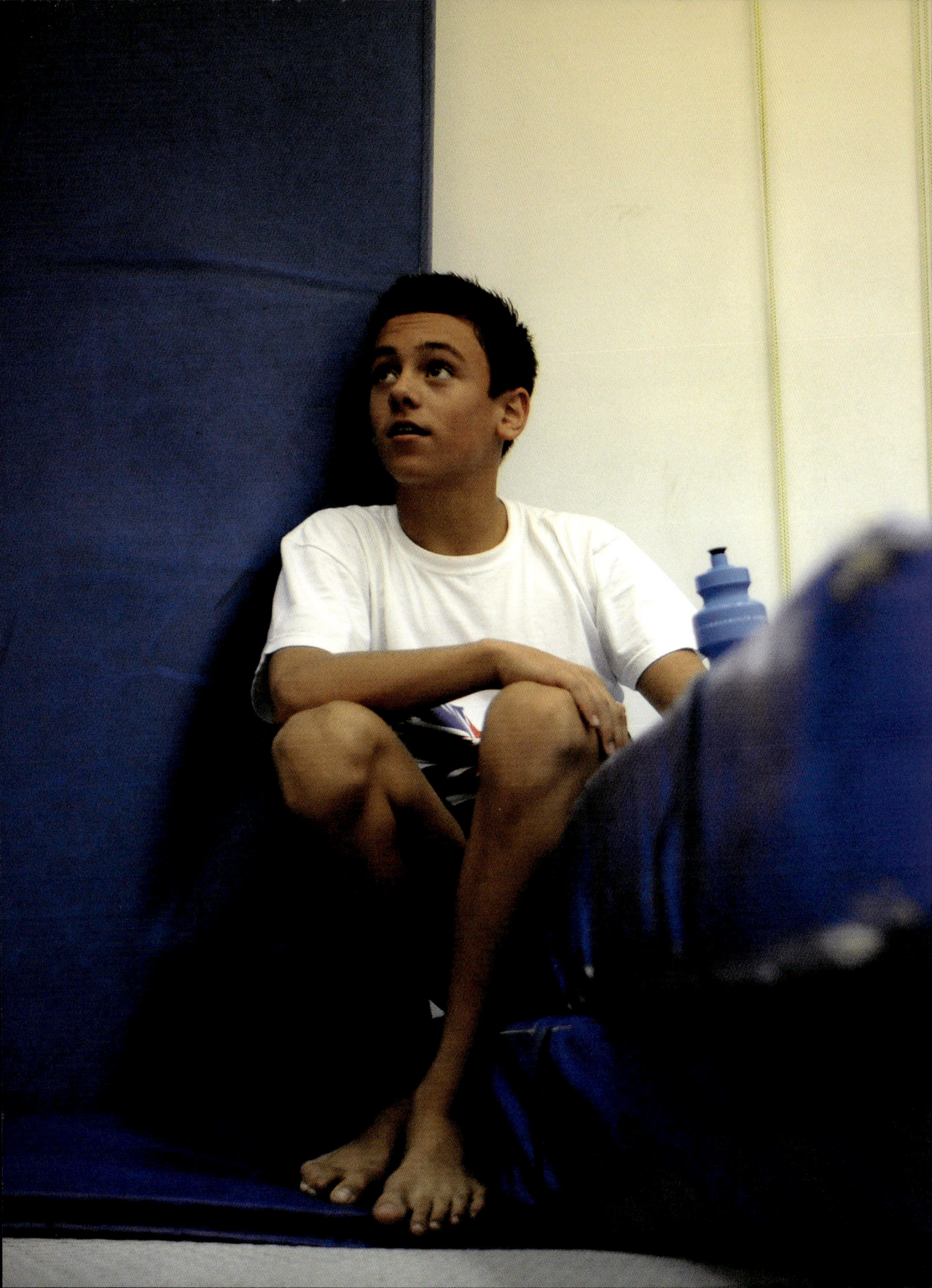

GOING
INTERNATIONAL

As my learning curve went vertical, I started to train more and more. In September 2003, I moved up to B Squad, where I trained on Mondays, Tuesdays and Thursdays from 6.30 p.m. to 7.30 p.m. in the gym and then from 7.30 p.m. to 8.30 p.m. in the pool. On Fridays I also trained from 4.15 p.m. to 5.45 p.m. in the pool and on Saturdays I had a dry-land session from 4 p.m. to 7 p.m. at Swallows, a gym nearby.

That month, I had another competition away from home – an invitational event in Southampton. I was homesick and cried every night but this time my parents were back in Plymouth and were not allowed to come down to see me. The managers had to be strict because it would be unfair to the other children if they made special allowances for me. I would sob down the phone, 'Come and get me, come and get me', but they just tried to talk me round. Poor Mum, sometimes I rang her ten or fifteen times a night. She always told me if I wanted to be part of the team, I needed to stick with them and that I would fall asleep if I tried. Eventually, of course, I would always drop off and wake up raring to go the next day.

Over that weekend, I picked up the gold in the 1m and 3m springboards and platform events. During these competitions away I always wanted to learn more and, when the rest of the team were given the option of returning to the hotel, I always wanted to stay and watch the other teams diving to absorb as much as I possibly could. Both Sam and Andy said I was like a sponge.

Later that month I started to perfect the front two and a half somersaults from 5m and a front two and a half somersaults piked from 3m.

At my next competition I had wins on the 1m, 3m and 5m platforms. On the 5m I scored 150.55 and the next competitor's score was 78.25 – so I was a long way ahead of my contemporaries. My enthusiasm was fired up even more and I relished the competitive element and the feeling of adrenalin when I stood with my feet touching the end of the diving board and everyone was silent, waiting for me to go. Rather than putting me off, the pressure just seemed to drive me on. I was awarded three shiny new medals and that week's 'Jubbly' said 'There seems to be no stopping him at the moment!'

I WAS LEARNING THAT, AS WELL AS THE PHYSICAL CHALLENGES, THERE ARE HUGE MENTAL HURDLES TO OVERCOME. ASIDE FROM THE ELEMENT OF FEAR, YOU HAVE SIX DIVES IN EVERY EVENT, SO IF YOU DO ONE BADLY, YOU HAVE TO PICK YOURSELF UP, FORGET ABOUT IT AND MOVE ON. IF YOU LET ONE BAD DIVE AFFECT THE REST OF THE COMPETITION THEN YOU HAVE LOST. YOU NEED TO BE MENTALLY TOUGH.

Sometimes if I did a bad dive when I was younger, I would scream, burst into tears and run off, knocking into anything, or anyone, who stood in my path. One day, at an Armada Cup competition, I was doing dives from the 1m springboard. During one I was doing the hurdle step and my knees gave way – I was trying to spin round but I hadn't got any height, so landed on my bum and got a failed dive. I stormed off poolside in a massive strop and sat in the fire exit, crying. In the end, one of the other divers, Claire Wonnacott, and my first weights coach – who we nicknamed Beef because he is a vegetarian – talked me round and I went back to the competition and came fourth in the end.

Andy had started coaching me by then because Sam had decided that she could not manage all the travelling and leaving her young baby at home. I remembered feeling disappointed when Sam announced that she would not be my coach any more, but we always saw her at the pool before she moved to Australia a couple of years later.

Andy taught me a new technique to deal with my nerves and the stress of competitions. He told me: 'Focus on happy thoughts like Peter Pan, so you can fly.' I slowly started to recognize bad feelings in the pit of my stomach, and would walk away and have a shower or a swim and come back thinking differently, otherwise I would be in a downward spiral. In competitions he could often tell if my concentration was going because I was worrying about what other people were doing – and he would tell me to start thinking about my next dive, focus on 'happy thoughts' and to ignore what everyone else was doing. After all, I could only control my own performance. That mentality is key to doing well. Dad always used to tell me never to compare myself to anyone else. Diving is not the sort of sport where you can liken yourself to someone else; you can only be in charge of your own dives.

In June I went to the National Championships in Southampton. Plymouth and Southampton were two of only seven 10m platforms in the country and, at the time, Southampton was considered one of the best facilities. I was starting to become unbeaten in my age group and I know now that they sent me to see how I would cope with the mental pressure of not winning. Everyone was expecting me to fail.

However, off I went and the nerves and tears never took hold, despite the fact that, while I had just turned ten, most of the divers I was up against were adults as old as thirty. On the first day was the 3m springboard and I came third in the under-18s and eighth in the senior competition. Dad was sobbing – he always cried when I did well. I always used to be a bit embarrassed, but now I think it's great he didn't care what anyone else thought. It just showed how proud he was of me. Mum is more the strong, silent type. I know that deep down she found it quite scary when I was up on the 10m board and was still so small.

FOR MY TENTH BIRTHDAY, IN MAY 2004, MUM AND DAD GOT ME A MASSIVE TRAMPOLINE TO GO IN THE GARDEN. I COULD ALWAYS PRACTISE THE SOMERSAULTS AND TWISTS I NEEDED FOR MY DIVING.

'I've got a bronze and it's not even my best board! I'm going to get a gold in platform,' I told Dad.

In the platform event the next day, I performed better than I ever had before. For this you can dive off 5m, 7m or 10m, but you are not supposed to dive off the top board until you are fourteen or fifteen. Looking back, they were really simple dives – a front two and a half piked off 7m, an inward two and a half somersaults with tuck off 7m, a back one and a half somersaults with tuck off 5m, a reverse one and a half piked off 1m and a back half off 7m. I finished my list with a simple armstand somersault.

I was learning fast about the importance of the list being right – lots of people had lists with higher tariffs but they didn't execute their dives as well. I was awarded a bronze in the senior competition and I became the youngest ever under-18 winner. I was also 50 points over the score needed by a twelve-year-old to qualify for the Junior Olympic Programme – but was still two years too young to qualify. I was delighted. Standing on the podium to collect my medal, I looked really funny – this tiny, skinny child next to the teenage gold and silver winners. I felt like a dwarf but after a while got used to the other competitors towering above me.

I also won the synchro, where I was partnered with another Plymouth diver, called Kyle Prior. We didn't train together at synchro when we were that age. The 1m boards at the Mayflower Centre are on the opposite ends of the pool, so we could not practise properly even if we wanted to. We just turned up and did it on the day. I loved the adventure and knew I would go back to my diving lessons more motivated than ever.

On the way home in the car, I kept asking Dad, 'When do you think I'll be in the *Herald*? I want to be in the paper!'

My wish was granted. The next day a small article appeared in our local paper with the headline, 'Diving Prodigy Daley is Youngest Ever UK Champion'. Mum showed it to me and I loved the thought that other people would be reading about me.

'MAYBE ONE DAY I'LL BE IN A NATIONAL NEWSPAPER,' I TOLD MY PARENTS. BUT THEY HAD NO IDEA WHAT LAY AHEAD AND KNEW NOTHING ABOUT ELITE COMPETITION, OR THAT THERE COULD BE A ROUTE FOR ME TO THE TOP OF THE SPORT.

Mum and Dad bought two copies of the local paper, one to laminate and an original and filed them away in the special file. Dad meticulously kept every single thing that was ever written about me in every newspaper and magazine, painstakingly filing and laminating and filing and laminating. We now have a whole garage filled with files.

We were at Watergate Bay when the 2004 Athens Olympics was on. I sat on the small sofa in our caravan and watched Leon Taylor and Pete Waterfield diving on the tiny portable TV set which we brought with us. We had to put the aerial on a broom handle so we could get some reception.

I was like a proper geek – I just sat there on my own as they jumped together in the synchro event, ripping their entries. I was particularly elated because when I had been in Southampton I had met Pete and asked him for his autograph. He signed my chamois with a marker pen.

PROUDLY WAVING MY GB FLAG WHILE THE 2004 OLYMPICS WERE ON – I WAS OBSESSED WITH THE DIVING.

Me and
Pete Waterfield
at the
Southampton
invitational
age: 10
2004

Me and
Chris Mears
on the
Podium at
the
Southampton
invitational
age: 10
2004
Me, Max,
Chris and
Kyle on the
Podium
for the
boys group
C platform
event
(me guest)
Won!
age: 10
2004

When we won a silver medal, I couldn't run fast enough to the clubhouse where my parents were, and drag them back to watch the medal ceremony and interviews afterwards. Watching the team grinning from ear to ear on the podium with the wreaths on their heads and medals round their necks, I was filled with enthusiasm thinking that one day maybe I could represent our country like they had.

And the Olympics, it seems, could be within my reach, because that October I was invited by Kim White to attend a Junior Olympic Programme camp in Southampton. I remember being a year younger than everyone else there and thinking it was cool to be with older people. Andy came to train me because two other Plymouth divers, Tonia Couch and Brooke Graddon, were also taking part. I went along and, much like the World Class Start camps, delighted in the diving, just not the being away from home and so, of course, there was the nightly round of pre-bed tears.

But my diving was still going from strength to strength and by the end of 2004 I was only beaten once in my age group and unbeaten for nine months.

I WAS WORKING HARDER THAN EVER BY THEN, TRAINING THREE HOURS A DAY, SIX DAYS A WEEK.

My frustration when my dives weren't perfect really drove me on. I was often tired in the morning and struggled to get up, but once I was out and throwing myself in the pool I was full of energy. Sometimes I was given the day off training after a meet, but would just turn up anyway after asking Dad to take me, hoping someone could give me some pointers. It felt like there was a fire burning in my belly.

Grandma Rose and Granddad Dink started to take me to training on a Wednesday night to give Dad a break but after a while he just used to come along and watch anyway.

He could not stay away! When I got a bit older we started going for a curry afterwards and have done that every Wednesday I have been at home since. I always look forward to it.

My first international competition was in Aachen, Germany, in April 2005. I was given special dispensation by the German Swimming Federation to compete – Kim White, the Junior Olympic Programme manager, persuaded them, even though the rules state that anyone born later than 1992 should be prevented from entering. Despite my win at the Nationals, the coaches really felt it would be a chance for me to see how it was to lose and to see how I would cope with it.

A few days before, there was a delivery at the door and it was my GB kit. I ripped open the package, which had a tracksuit, T-shirts, shorts, a hat and drinks bottle. It was a really proud moment and I know Mum and Dad felt the same. I loved it. Now when I get new kit through it goes straight in the washing machine, but then I tried on every single item of clothing to make sure it fitted and walked up and down to see if it was comfortable. I wore it all to training at the first possible opportunity. That's when my fascination with GB flags really started. I made my dad try for ages to find a pair of trunks with a Union Jack on them and now my room is full of Union Jack paraphenalia.

While I flew over with the rest of the team a few days before the competition for a training camp, Mum and Dad made the long drive in the car with my Grandma Rose. Despite my homesickness, the governing body was responsible for my welfare and I didn't stay in the same hotel as Mum and Dad. While I am at competitions, I am in the care of British Swimming. It felt strange at first but now I am used to it. I spoke to them really regularly on the phone and felt comforted by the fact they were in a hotel nearby. Dad kept saying to me that I was on the international circuit now and even if I came last I would have done amazingly well. Speaking to him always made me feel like whatever happened it would not matter, and however I did, it would always be good enough.

The facilities, which included a state-of-the-art dry-land area right on the poolside, were incredible. As the event started, I was in awe of the other divers, who all seemed to be ripping their dives. There were team coaches from all the countries and a much bigger and noisier crowd, different groups of people with every team and lots of foreign voices. There was a real buzz in the air and the whole building was filled with excitement and anticipation. My first event was the 3m springboard. I had a hard list for my age and felt nervous. I had butterflies and my heart was hammering but as I stood, poised to take my dives, I remembered what Sam and Andy said, that I should try and turn my nerves into energy. I reminded myself that if I thought happy thoughts I would fly.

me with
my medals
I won in
Aachen
2005
age:10
2005

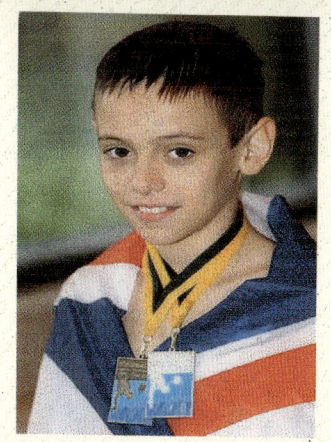

me with
the bent
legs doing
an inward
1½ on 7.5m
age:10 2005

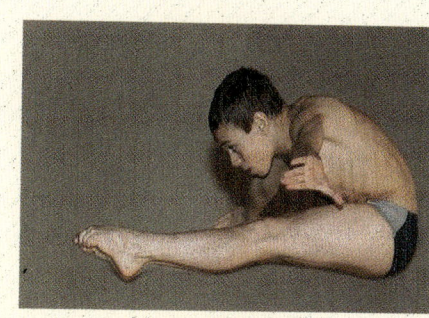

me climbing
outen of
the pool
with my
medals on
age:10 2005

me doing
a back
dive
straight
age:10
2005

front
+1½ som.
on 7.5m
2005
age:10

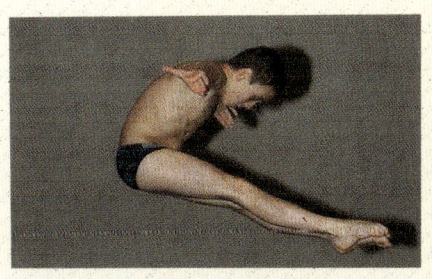

I've never really clicked with springboard. You need to spend time on it and I've always preferred the excitement of the higher platforms and the feeling of plummeting down into the water. I was never springboard-orientated, and do not think I was ever really seen as a 3m diver, but I concentrated hard and still qualified for the final. After I had completed my list in the final, I sat on the side of the pool with the chamois round my neck, transfixed by the leader board. My name stayed there and more and more divers kept going but I remained in the top three and eventually, it was only the two Chinese divers who came ahead of me. I could not believe it had happened. Dad was jumping up and down hugging everyone. I could see him in the crowd because he had bought a new, huge Union Jack, which he always waved at every competition from then so I knew where he was in the stands. I felt absolutely elated. It's the first time that I showed my competitive streak coming through and, rather than buckling under the pressure, being on the bigger stage only served to push me harder.

In the prelim of the platform event, I scraped into the final in twelfth place after a Russian guy made an error. I knew I needed to up my game and, charged with adrenalin, I went for it, scoring a 9. My first 9 in my first international competition! I only missed my reverse two and a half somersaults with tuck off the 7m board and I was beaten to second place by five points.

People started to make a fuss of me. I can remember Andy saying that loads of the other coaches had come up to him and asked him about our training and what his next moves were for me. Then sometimes other divers would ask for photos because they thought I might do well in the upcoming years. I felt fantastic. But I was starting to learn a familiar pattern and after these big events, as soon as I got home, it was back to reality and back to school, homework and training as normal.

After the Aachen competition, I received a £10,000 scholarship via TASS, the Talented Athlete Sponsorship Scheme designed to help athletes they felt could win a medal in 2012. I was the youngest of 107 athletes from thirty-four sports, including a disabled swimmer, a judoist, a modern pentathlete and a speed skater, all of whom were fourteen or fifteen. I was chuffed to get it, but was so young I didn't really think about the financial side of things. When you're that age, you just take everything at face value. I never knew how much it was or really understood what it was but I knew it meant that my family could come with me to support me at every competition. While I was taken with British Swimming they have never had any financial support to travel around, so I was happy about it.

Not long after that, I also received my first bit of fan mail from a Chinese diver called Urs Yu Zhou. It was on pretty paper with lots of stickers and she told me she was trying to improve her English so she could write to me more. Dad, delighted at my new-found fame in China, where they worship divers, duly laminated it and put it in the most recent diving file.

I continued competing and going to camps and by May 2005 I had been unbeaten in my own age group since November 2003. I never felt complacent though and wanted to continue pushing myself harder and harder – and felt satisfied when I learnt new dives and perfected old ones. It's really difficult to be up front. It is much easier to be chasing the top spot than it is to maintain that position because you need to have targets and Sam and Andy wanted me to have goals to reach for. The next stop was the mighty 10m platform, the big daddy of all the diving boards.

CLIMBING HIGHER
AND HIGHER

I went up to the 10m board for the first time just before I turned eleven. Normally you are not allowed to dive from there until you are at least twelve because of the risk of damaging your growing joints, but I had mastered everything I could off the lower boards and Andy knew I needed to keep learning and that he needed to keep challenging me in case I got bored or my interest started to wane. And he always knew that I could move quickly in the air, so if I got into trouble I could turn myself or correct my position so I entered the water vertically. He calls it my 'get out of jail free' card.

CLIMBING UP THE FINAL TWO SETS OF LADDERS I PRACTICALLY CRAWLED TO THE END. AS I GOT FURTHER ALONG, IT FELT LIKE THE BOARD WAS GETTING NARROWER AND LIKE I WAS WALKING ON A BALANCE BEAM AND COULD FALL OFF EITHER SIDE. THE POOL LOOKED LIKE A SHEET OF GLASS. I WAS TERRIFIED.

Andy just told me to jump off and after five minutes of talking myself into it, I leaped. It felt like I was flying and when I hit the water and got sucked under, it didn't hurt. In the same session I did my favourite dive, an inward two and a half piked off the 10m. As I landed with a rip, I smiled under the water. I felt so proud afterwards and ecstatic about finally getting up there. Before long I was learning one of the harder dives, a forward three and a half piked from the top platform.

At the Central Park Pool, your dive is filmed and played back on a screen behind the boards with a fifteen-second delay. Back then, it was cool to watch your dive from the mighty 10m block, run back up the stairs and do another one and watch it back. Now it is far more useful because we analyse it and see what we have done wrong and how we can improve. It's got more and more useful as the years have gone by.

There is always the worry of us growing in growth spurts because it puts us at increased risk of injury. At WCS camps I was measured to help identify if I would grow. I was still small at 4ft 6in, weighing just 4 stone 10lb. Being short is a good thing for divers because it means you can move quicker through the air. For a long time I wore strong black wrist supports so I didn't hurt my wrist joints when I dived, because my hands always take the brunt of the impact. I was limited in the number of dives from 10m I did in each session to about six, so the impact on my growing bones and joint plates wasn't too much. I still can't to do too many but often do up to eighteen dives from the top board in one day.

My first big trip away was to Perth for the Australian Junior Elite Diving Championship in July 2005. I had just turned eleven.

We stayed in beachside apartments and one day on the beach there were giant waves that reached over my head. We were all running in and out of the surf, but while everyone else was being knocked over as the waves crashed against the sand, I found a way to dive through them and get out further and further into the sea.

The adults were yelling at me to come back and I shouted back that they needed to come and catch me. They tried to run after me but kept getting knocked down!

Outside our training, they tried to keep us happily amused. We went to the zoo, where I saw kangaroos and koalas for the first time. I really suffered with jet lag, though, and some days I would just fall asleep at the table, or even under it. I was so small, the other divers would just leave me.

I shared a room with Max Brick and Charles Calvert, who I have always got on well with. Other Plymouth teammates, like Tonia and Brooke, who are now both fantastic friends, were there too. I think all the other kids probably got a bit annoyed by me because I was so homesick. I would call my mum every night – of course, it was in the middle of the day at home – and beg her to pick me up but she would just tell me that by the time she got out to Australia it would be the morning for me and I would have gone to sleep and woken up for a new day. Looking back, I think it was really hard for her too. I used to sit up all night doing crosswords, hugging my lucky monkey and thinking about going back home to my bedroom in Plymouth, until I would eventually drop off to sleep.

We would eat out most nights while we were in Perth and on one particular evening we were eating dinner at an Italian restaurant.

THE ANNOUNCEMENT ABOUT WHO WAS GOING TO HOST THE OLYMPICS IN 2012 WAS IMMINENT.

London, Madrid, Paris, New York and Moscow were the candidates. Kim White, the team manager, kept picking up his mobile phone, asking how things were going. At the end of the meal, his phone buzzed and a hushed silence fell over the table.

Snaps from my scrapbook.

AS HE PICKED IT UP, HIS FACE LIT UP. 'WE'VE GOT IT!' HE YELLED. EVERYONE WAS CHEERING AND CRYING.

I was the only one not crying. I had to force out some tears. How awful would that be – I'd spent every single night crying up until then and finally we had a reason to cry! I had not really comprehended what it meant at that point. I have since read that when the news came, I started crying because 'I could foresee my destiny', but sadly that's not exactly how it happened!

Towards the end of the week, I took gold on the platform event with a score of 418.98, with Charles Calvert and his teammate Callum Johnstone taking bronze and silver. I lost my lucky monkey while we were away and was devastated. The day after my individual was the synchro event, where I competed again with Kyle. We were in first place all the way through until one of the last dives, where I got to the end of the board and forgot what I was doing. Next thing I knew Kyle was in the water and I was still on the board, so I just plopped in after him. I got failed dive and was convinced it was because I had lost my monkey. When I got home the sports psychologist tried to tell me that the monkey wasn't lucky, but just a comfort blanket and I needed to be able to dive without

it, but I was still so upset. A few days later, Mum said she found it, but I think she might have gone out and bought me a new one. I didn't care – my lucky monkey was back!

When I arrived home from the airport, Dad took me strawberry picking so we could spend some proper time together and because he had missed me so much. He told me it was OK to eat some, as long as they didn't have any green worms in them, and to put some in my pocket and face the sun. As I turned, squinting into the sunlight, he squashed all the fruit in my pocket! You never knew when he was being serious. Later we went fishing in Babbacombe, just the two of us, and he caught a garfish. He then told us we were going to take it home and eat it and I had a strop, saying I didn't like fish. He smacked it on the wall a couple of times, until it was completely lifeless!

Dad was still working full-time at that point. He had taken over the business where he worked making special-purpose machines supporting large, high-volume manufacturing companies. He would go to work at 7 a.m., rush home to pick me up to take me training and then go home again.

HE JOKED THAT HE WAS 'TAXI DRIVER DAD' – BUT HE HAD CAUGHT THE BUG TOO AND WAS DELIGHTED WHEN I DID WELL, ALWAYS CRIED, AND WAS FOREVER KEEN TO TAKE PART AND HELP OUT AT THE DIVING CLUB WHEN HE COULD, WHETHER IT WAS FERRYING US AROUND OR DRESSING UP AS ELVIS AND SANTA AT THE PARTIES. HE WAS ALWAYS BY MY SIDE AND HE WAS PRACTICALLY PART OF THE FURNITURE AT THE MAYFLOWER CENTRE.

As well as carefully keeping all my certificates and press cuttings, he started to video all my competitions with a camcorder and tripod and hung all the medals I won in my bedroom. He measured out all the nails so they were perfectly distanced, although when the windows are open they sound like wind chimes.

In October, I was the youngest person ever to compete in a series of optional dives off 10m, and in November I first started getting interest from TV programmes and everyone started to talk about Britain's Olympic hopes for 2012. I had wanted to be on the TV after being in a few newspapers so was super-excited. The BBC started following me around for a programme and at first it was a bit weird being on camera, but because I was so young I didn't really notice and soon got used to it. One day they came into school. The others kids were waving at their mums, pulling stupid faces in front of the camera and being silly. It seemed monumentally important who I chose to be in the classroom with me when the cameras were rolling. Everyone was saying, 'Choose me, choose me!' and if I didn't, then they would not talk to me for the rest of the day.

The media attention was really starting to pick up – and there was a growing buzz about London 2012.

The *Daily Mail* picked seven athletes as its 'Magnificent Seven' – planning to follow us in the seven years up to the Olympic games. The other six were BMX racer Shanaze Reade, runner Emily Pidgeon, gymnast Louis Smith, sailor Giles Scott, judo competitor Jean-Rene Badrick and swimmer Rachel Latham. And not long after I was asked to be part of the *Daily Mail* scheme, I was nominated for the first time for BBC Young Sports Personality of the Year. As each opportunity presented itself I just wanted to grab it; I loved the attention and recognition for doing something I was so passionate about. Every

time something new came along, it came as a surprise for both my parents and me but we lapped it up.

WE STARTED TO GET INTO A ROUTINE, SO MUM WAS THE CHIEF ORGANIZER, PLANNING OUR DIARIES AND DOING GENERAL MUM JOBS LIKE COOKING AND CLEANING, AND DAD WOULD FERRY ME AROUND TO TRAINING AND ALL MY MEDIA AND SPONSORSHIP EVENTS.

Dad would also help with William and Ben and Mum would give him a list at the start of every day of various pick-up times for all of us and our various after-school activities.

A couple of months later, the *Daily Mail* took the seven of us for the first time, with our parents, to see the Olympic Park being built in London. Dad and I piled onto a bus, where a special guide talked us through what was being built and where. To me, it just looked like loads of soil and mounds of mud – and the guide was talking about washing the soil in special machines and moving the 20,000 newts from one pond to another. It was when the man got around to the bit in his speech about one area being important for a certain species of bat that both Dad and I nodded off.

ABOVE

Checking out the Olympic Park. Sadly there wasn't that much to see.

DOING MY
USUAL TRAINING,
BUT THIS TIME
WEARING
SOMETHING
DIFFERENT!

In December, I was named *Evening Herald* Young Sports Personality of the Year. Andy had won Coach of the Year, Brooke had won Top Amateur Sports Personality and the diving team had won Team of the Year. My whole family came, including both sets of grandparents, aunts and uncles, and loads of our friends – we had about eighteen tickets between us and two huge tables.

DAD WAS SO HAPPY AND PROUD OF ME HE DRANK HIS BEER OUT OF MY GLASS TROPHY. I REMEMBER NOT BEING TOO HAPPY ABOUT THAT.

Around then, Leon Taylor was asked by British Swimming to be my mentor. He was a major diving icon after his Olympic win in 2004 and he was someone I really looked up to. He came to see me training in Plymouth and rang me quite often to see how my training was going. He always asked loads of questions about our competitions, what I was learning and how I was feeling. He was always so enthusiastic and it was great to have someone else to talk to who totally understood my worries.

As the attention ramped up, my diving seemed to get better and better. The first time I was due to compete against Leon was at the ASA (Amateur Swimming Association) National Championships at the Manchester Aquatics Centre in December. It was also the Commonwealth Games qualifier – and I needed 390 points to get to the Games the following year. I was really eager to be competing against Leon for the challenge but he ended up dropping out because of a bad knee and I was really gutted. I was starting to flourish more and more in competitions and for the first time scored five perfect 10s, one more than Peter Waterfield, the British Number One at that time, two for my front three and a half somersaults with tuck, two for inward two and half somersaults with tuck and one for my backward two and a half somersaults with one and a half twists. They were my first 10s in a senior competition. Weirdly, I got my lowest scores for the easiest dives. My score of 399.05 made me eligible to compete at the Commonwealths. I was really happy, although I didn't really know what it meant and whether I would be allowed to go, but Dad was ecstatic. He was sobbing with tears of happiness and gave me a giant bear hug when I saw him. He was never afraid to show his emotions because he was always very open.

HE WAS SAYING: 'OH MY GOD, YOU'VE DONE IT. YOU'VE DONE IT.'

I was still really young and new to the international circuit, so in the end it was decided that I was too young to go and that Leon would go instead. I wasn't worried or disappointed and Dad promised me we could go out to watch. I was on a complete high.

Dad and I went out to watch the Commonwealth Games at the Melbourne Aquatics Centre in March 2006. We were there for about ten days and stayed at a hotel which overlooked the Melbourne Grand Prix course.

I also remember Dad getting this surf and turf meal one day, which consisted of crocodile, kangaroo and shark. Then one day at breakfast, I avoided the sausages because they looked really white and horrible and when I took a closer look they were ostrich sausages. When I told Dad, he was horrified and didn't go near them again!

The competition crowd was huge and I think I would have been really scared and overwhelmed. In the end, Leon didn't dive because of an injury but it was good to watch and we really enjoyed ourselves. I was dressed in my red and white T-shirt and hat and cheered really loudly

for the Brits. Pete got a silver medal in the platform event and the Brits Tony Ally and Mark Shipman also won silver in the 3m synchro. On one day when we were watching the diving, Dad and I didn't have very good seats so Tony Ally put me on his shoulders and pretended I was his son and walked me up into the athletes' seating area, so I had a better view.

I felt so excited about what I was accomplishing and that I could carve out a future for myself in diving.

One day during a normal training session after school, I was on the 5m board doing a dive involving one and a half twists, but somehow I put in two and a half. I did it twice by mistake, went up for a third attempt, thought about it and then came down and went into a panic. I didn't understand why I was doing it and felt really disorientated. Then a week later I landed flat from 10m. I was going through a really bad patch because I'd grown a lot and that makes it hard to make technical changes quickly, or it can make you uncoordinated because your body is learning to work around a new centre of gravity. My arms felt longer and it was confusing. One day I hit my feet on the board and on another I had landed painfully flat on my back. I put these occasions down as just blips and carried on, telling myself that everyone had setbacks from time to time and it was because I was growing. I hoped it would be OK and I would go back to diving like I had been before.

It was decided that in April I would go back to compete in Aachen in Germany, where I'd won silver previously. Mum and Dad and my brothers drove over. Because they had started to do a lot of travelling, my Uncle Kevin's firm, Airtech, gave us a Volkswagen Transporter to drive with free petrol, which was great. It helped so much.

At the event, it was like the year before: the same big international crowds, high standards and competitive vibes. After doing my first two dives from 10m, which were fine and normal, I climbed the stairs to take my third. About halfway up, I went blank and froze. My head felt fuzzy; I didn't know what I was doing. I thought I had forgotten the movements and would lose myself in the air. I was petrified. I had to walk back down the steps.

Andy wasn't there but I went over to the team manager and told him I didn't want to compete any more. I think he thought I might pull myself out of it so, as a test, told me I had to walk up one of the ladders and tell the recorders. My name had not been called by that point, but it was while I was talking to the recorder, telling him I wanted to pull out, that my name was called. I got really upset and by the time I made it to my family I felt humiliated and so guilty that they had driven all the way there.

'You don't want to try, no?' Dad asked me gently.

I shook my head. I felt totally overwhelmed. It felt so strange that the year before I had been so happy and excited, while this time it was the complete opposite. I could not understand what had happened and why I was feeling so scared. I just wanted my diving to go back to how it was before.

I DIDN'T GO UP ON THE 10M AFTER THAT COMPETITION FOR ABOUT NINE MONTHS. I JUST FELT I COULDN'T DO IT. I HAD LOST MY NERVE AND AS FAR AS I WAS CONCERNED MY DIVING CAREER WAS OVER.

LEARNING TO FACE MY FEARS

THE WEEK WE CAME BACK FROM GERMANY, I ARRIVED HOME FROM A NORMAL DAY AT SCHOOL AND DAD HAD SHAVED HIS BROWN MOP OF HAIR OFF AND WAS COMPLETELY BALD.

'I've got a fiver from everyone in the pub to shave my head for Comic Relief,' he said, grinning. It didn't sound strange because it was around the time of Comic Relief's Red Nose Day and I didn't think twice.

The next day, he wasn't at home when my brother and I came in from school, which was unusual. Mum and Grandma Rose were at home and told us that he'd gone to hospital for some check-ups. We all accepted that and piled into the car to the hospital.

At the hospital room, he was lying on the bed with a massive white bandage around his head. Ben had had an operation when he was two and hated hospitals. He was only five and really terrified. He sat outside crying and refused to go in and see him.

'He's got a really bad headache, that's why he's got a bandage on,' Mum told us. But it didn't make sense, and when I went to sit by his hospital bed, he looked really poorly. Dad kept calling the bandage his 'turban', insisting he was fine.

'This turban means I'm changing religions,' Dad said with a big smile. 'It's just some check-ups. All completely normal and routine.'

At home, when William and Ben were in bed, I started asking more questions.

'He's just got a poorly head,' Grandma insisted.

I'd heard of cancer and knew that is was a Bad Thing, so I just came out with it.

'He hasn't got cancer, has he?'

'He's got a little thing growing in his head. It's a tumour.'

'A tumour,' I thought. 'At least it's not cancer.'

Dad spent about ten days in hospital and then he went to Grandma's house to recuperate because it was quieter there. When he came back home we were told we needed to be gentle with him and couldn't bundle him on the sofa, this thing we used to do all the time where we piled on top of each other. Mum would sometimes get involved and perch herself on the top of the pile, too!

But that rough-and-tumble stuff was strictly off limits while he was recovering, we were told.

I knew he started to have radiotherapy but never really understood completely what it meant. At the time I thought it was daily check-ups and we never went with him to the hospital because we were at school. I never saw Mum or Grandma crying, so I never realized the seriousness of it. He was always the same old dad, joking and messing around all the time and taking me everywhere in the car. I never felt scared; I took it for granted that he would get better. Everyone did.

I now know that for three years before he'd been having panic attacks for about thirty seconds to a minute each time. They would be completely random – he would get them at home and sometimes when he was driving. Mum and Dad tried to shield me from his illness but, even then, I could sometimes tell the difference when he was snappy or short-tempered because he was so worried about himself. He had decided to give up his job months earlier after the doctor told him the episodes were down to stress. Often he said he felt like he was hallucinating, like his head was filling up with water. He kept going back to our GP, over and over again, but they just told him to relax and not to worry. They even sent him to a psychiatrist, who told him there was nothing wrong with his mental health and recommended that he should go for a scan.

The tumour was the size of a grapefruit and he was told the day before my competition in Aachen, where I had pulled out. He was advised not to go out to Germany but his reasoning was that he had had the thing in his head for months, so a week would not make any difference. I wonder now whether I sensed he was ill, even if I didn't realize it, and that's why things had also gone spectacularly wrong there. The doctors cut out 80 per cent of the tumour but the rest of it was too dangerous to remove because it was connected to nerve endings.

DAD WAS CONSTANTLY UPBEAT. HE KEPT SAYING THAT HE NEVER FELT ANY PAIN AND WAS MORE SCARED OF GOING TO THE DENTIST THAN THE HOSPITAL. HE ALWAYS SAW THE POSITIVE IN EVERYTHING AND NEVER SHOWED BEN, WILLIAM AND ME THAT HE WAS WORRIED.

The fact that it might have been cancer was always in the back of my mind and as time went on I started to think more and more that it could be. I cannot remember exactly how I found out properly; I think I probably overheard a conversation in the kitchen. But I didn't really think twice. I thought it was cool that Dad had beaten it and was so strong.

After he got his first set of results saying the tumour had shrunk, he hosted a 'Rob's still here' party at a room in a pub down the road, where we raised money for a local hospice. About 250 of our family and friends came along. It was five people deep at the bar and he got so drunk that he threw up and had to come home early. In later years, each December, he had a 'Rob's still here' party. It was always one of the highlights of the year for everyone and I know Dad loved having everyone together in one place having fun.

I WAS STILL GOING THROUGH A HORRIBLE TIME WITH MY DIVING AND WAS CONSTANTLY SCARED AND NERVOUS. I TOLD ANDY: 'MY DIVING CAREER'S FINISHED. I CAN NEVER GO BACK ON THE HIGH BOARDS BECAUSE I DON'T KNOW WHERE I AM, AND THAT'S IT.'

Andy showed me quickly that that wasn't the case. He organized a Chinese coach to talk me through the problem and then spoke to the sports psychologist at British Diving, Michele Miller, who had helped me through my homesickness before.

He then encouraged me to speak to the likes of the gymnast Beth Tweddle, who I was friends with on Facebook. She told me that it wasn't uncommon and I could get over it. She had overcome it herself and in sports like gymnastics, trampolining and diving, which are all quite similar, a lot of people suffered from the problem of feeling they were losing themselves in the air, but with time and patience they beat it. Sam Grevett and Kim White also got involved – everyone was willing me and helping me to overcome my problem. I had a massive support system.

I discovered the experience is called Lost Movement Syndrome. The complexity and difficulty of the routine must be matched by the quality of mental preparation because this creates the pathways or instructions for the body to subsequently follow. The clearer the mental preparation, the better the outcome. And if you're tired or unfocused, your brain becomes confused because you are moving at such a high speed and the mental pathways may not be etched clearly or distinctly enough. Your instinct, always on the alert to keep you from damage, pain and harm, reads this confusion as trouble, and sends out warning messages. Panic then floods your system. The mental pathways between mind and body, which should be clear, become lost in the flood. This is what had happened to me in Aachen and the trust between me and my instinct was broken and my confidence shattered.

Slowly, I calmed down and started to think maybe everything had been moving too quickly. We needed to strip it all back down to basics again, so we started to rebuild the dives and the 'schemas' in my brain. Andy told me: 'I call it a Grand Canyon in the head. As you learn a movement pattern, your brain will remember it. If it's the wrong one, you have to dig up one canyon and dig another channel.'

To rebuild the dive, we had to reinforce the schemas and get the canyon going the right way again. We started from the basics on the dry-land and in the pool, in the rig and out of the rig. At the lower boards, he added one twist – one schema – then went higher up the boards and, over a number of months, we gradually built in more height, more twists and somersaults, putting together a skill chain, a connection of schemas so that they all hung together. Everything was in place for me to rebuild my confidence and my dives.

IT WAS A REAL LOW POINT FOR ME HAVING PROGRESSED VERY QUICKLY UNTIL THEN. I FOUND THE PROCESS SLOW AND FRUSTRATING. I FELT BROKEN AND MY CONFIDENCE WAS AT AN ALL-TIME LOW.

I was sensitive around Tonia and Brooke, the other divers in the top team at Central Park Pool, who would tell me to get on with it and I would be fine. They had never experienced anything like it at that point and didn't understand how I felt. I would often find myself bursting into tears when I got into the car after a training session. It felt so mentally draining and I was constantly tired. Dad always seemed to know when I was particularly knackered and would tell me to go to bed early, which I did, but I still found myself exhausted from school and training. I continued to work hard at rebuilding my diving and my confidence and continued to go on training camps. In October, I went to China for the first time with World Class Start. We stayed at a school and trained every day. I was homesick again and didn't want to stay there and struggled to get to sleep because of jetlag. My team manager came up with this technique whereby he told me to try and stay awake and when I tried to keep my eyes open I would always end up dropping off. China was really different to how I imagined. It was quite a strange experience, especially when it came to the food. I thought it would be Chinese takeaways every night, but it was canteen food. One night they offered us dog for dinner, the next night cat soup and then another night lamb brains was on the menu. I didn't even realize then that you could eat that kind of stuff. On the last day we saw they had put out chips and we were so excited and piled our plates really high. Sitting down, eager to tuck in and finally have some proper food, I had one bite and realized they were cold with sugar on. It was horrible. I just ate rice, cabbage and sweetcorn and came back so skinny.

Back at home I was starting to make good progress and everything slowly started to click back into place. Each time I did a good dive, I felt slightly better, until I finally made it back up on the 10m around December and it was like I had never been off it. It didn't feel like a huge deal being back up there and because we had gone back to basics I found that my technique was better. I was stronger, calmer and more confident.

I learned that I had been given special dispensation to compete at the Australian Youth Olympic Festival in Sydney, despite being two years below the minimum age. I was really proud and pleased about the decision. It was a proper Olympic event with an opening ceremony and an athletes' parade and the national anthems were played when people won events.

One day in training, I grabbed my hands too hard when I hit the water and I painfully bent my thumb backwards. It was really sore and in the end we made a cast to keep it in a secure place, which helped. I had a scan on it and if I had broken it I would have had to wear a cast for weeks and would have been unable to dive. I started to realize for the first time how easy it is to be set back and I was very upset because

I didn't think I would make it to Australia – Mum and Dad had already paid out for them and William and Ben to come and watch me and Grandma had also booked her ticket. I dived feet first for three weeks and hoped for the best.

My diving was back on track, but I still felt apprehensive. Andy kept me thinking positive and told me to enjoy myself, which I did. In a Christmas card he had written me, he praised me for the way I had got over the setback and then wrote: 'Keep smiling and enjoy your job – just another day in the office! You have one extra-strong thumb – remember the positive thinking.' His cards always made me smile and feel really motivated. It had been a particularly tough year but he made me feel good about what I had achieved.

I did make it out to Australia in January 2007. My thumb was still painful but I soldiered on. I could not spend that much time with my family, because I was always expected to be with the team and even though I was the youngest, it would have been unfair on the others if I had been allowed time out with them. My family had an amazing holiday outside of watching the events I was competing in and they did all the normal touristy things, like going to the Sydney Harbour Bridge and to the zoo.

While it was my first competition back on the 10m and I felt shaky, I also felt more confident and finished fourth after being beaten by three Chinese divers. My list was quite simple after the setbacks. Afterwards, Andy told me we would start relearning my inward three and a half somersaults and other higher degree of difficulty dives, like my back armstand triple somersaults with tuck. I was nervous and resistant at first.

'IT'S SIMPLE TOM. IF YOU WANT TO KEEP COMING FOURTH THEN YOU CAN STICK WITH THE CURRENT LIST,' HE TOLD ME. 'BUT IF YOU WANT TO IMPROVE AND GET BACK INTO THE MEDALS THEN YOU NEED TO UP YOUR GAME.'

Fourth is a particularly frustrating place to be, especially when there are only a few points in it. That comment was enough to make me want to start learning those dives again!

In the synchro, I had started partnering Callum Johnstone, who trained in Leeds. For synchro competitions there are normally eleven judges: two groups of three judges score one of the divers each in the execution of the dive, making a total of six scores for the pair, while five judges score the synchronization of the dive. The high and the low score for each diver in execution is dropped, leaving two scores, and the highest and lowest of the five synchronization scores are dropped leaving three scores to be added together. These are then added to the execution scores and multiplied by the degree of difficulty and then 0.6 to give the total award on the dive. It's quite confusing. But you always have a good idea of where you are during the event from the scores.

I liked not being up on the boards alone. It felt good to share the moment with someone and it's all about teamwork. The training does not differ because it's exactly the same routines and again we had not done much together beforehand. Partners are put together when they are naturally matched and fall and rotate at the same speeds and Callum was more than a foot taller than me but we dived well together and came second in the final. It was our first international together, so we were really happy.

When I came home we went on a big family skiing holiday to Ellmau in

ONE OF THE DOWNSIDES TO MY TRAINING IS THAT I'M NOT ALLOWED TO SKI – REALLY GUTTING AS I USED TO LOVE IT!

Austria with Mum, Dad, William and Ben, Grandma Rose and Granddad Dink, Uncle Jamie and Aunty Debbie, my cousins Dylan and Todd, Aunty Marie and Uncle Jason, and my cousin Malia, who was a baby then. All the kids went off to ski school every morning and we absolutely loved it. One of my best memories from that holiday was after one of the youngsters complained that I won all the trophies and they never won anything, Granddad Dink bought William, Ben, my cousins Dylan and Todd, and me silver trophies with each of our names engraved on them. He then pretended that he had been told to give them out for winning races at ski school. I went along with it. All my family never treat me differently and we are all made to feel special for our separate achievements.

My first big sponsorship came in the form of Visa, whose team were out in Sydney. When I got home they asked me to be part of Team Visa, where athletes are mentored by multi-medal-winners Dame Tanni Grey-Thompson and Sir Steve Redgrave. It was a real honour to be asked. I just had to agree to make five public appearances, including opening shopping centres and autograph sessions, which I was more than happy to take part in. We were invited to a few days in London, where we were told about our role within the team and were introduced to the media. I had not been to London before then.

Both Tanni and Steve were lovely and really helpful. They both gave us their phone numbers and email addresses in case we had any questions for them.

Steve told us: 'We are open all hours. We have been joking about being called at two in the morning, but if that does happen, I won't be annoyed. I'll know it's about an issue you need to talk about.'

ABOVE

My first trip to London.

He also talked to us about expectation and the fact that each event we would do would be different, and described how he struggled mentally at one Olympics more than at the others. He said the difference between winning and losing was down to strength of mind and wanted to pass on advice about how to cope with the level of training and expectation before big events. I made everybody laugh by telling them that it was my ambition to break Steve's record of winning five Olympic gold medals. I'm regretting that now!

BELOW

Mum and Dad

all glammed up

for a day out.

Privately, I spoke to him about a number of things, like how he felt about competitions. He also reassured me that while sometimes training would be hard and relentless, it would pay off in the end. He was particularly helpful when I said I was worried about being unable to sleep before major competitions. He told me that our bodies can still perform on a lot less sleep than we are sometimes used to. That really reassured me and therefore I started to get to sleep a lot easier.

Leon advised me to get an agent because other opportunities might be available to me. A lady called Natasha helped me get a sponsorship contract with Adidas, which has been ongoing. When the first set of kit arrived, it was like Christmas. I got loads of different tops and tracksuits in my size but it was great because William and Ben got the odd pair of trainers. Around six months later, I switched agents to Professional Sports Group after they secured me a deal with the healthy school food brand, Sodexo. A team was starting to build around me and it felt good.

QUALIFYING
FOR BEIJING

AT THE START OF 2007, THERE WAS A VERY REAL CHANCE
I COULD MAKE IT TO THE BEIJING OLYMPICS THE FOLLOWING
YEAR AND ANDY HAD DEVISED A PROGRAMME TO HELP ME
PROGRESS. HE DIDN'T TELL ME TOO MUCH ABOUT IT IN
ADVANCE – IT WAS MORE ON A 'NEED TO KNOW' BASIS, SO
I DIDN'T FEEL SCARED OR OVERWHELMED.

Everyone was keen for me to get some more experience and
exposure on the bigger stage if I was to stand a chance of qualifying
for the Olympics. They wanted to build my experience up slowly, so
that year I also started on the FINA Grand Prix Series, which was
my biggest step so far on the international circuit. It is a series of six
or seven meets each year that feature men's and women's 3m and
10m synchro and individual events. In each one you can accumulate
points and become the overall winner, and aside from the Olympics
and Commonwealth Games these are the biggest events on the
globe because you are up against every country's top divers.

I made my FINA debut in Montreal, Canada, at the end of April, guided
by Andy and the British National Diving Performance Director, Steve
Foley. I was competing against the world's best divers – Olympic,
Commonwealth and European champions. They were looking for a top
twelve finish. If I managed that Steve said it would be 'outstanding' and
he would be happy. My best dive was my armstand back triple with
tuck and I beat the qualifying standard and came tenth with 395.95.
Everyone was delighted.

After the promising start, during the second week of June I flew out to
the FINA event in Madrid, where I started to compete with a harder list
of dives. I was diving against more top divers, including China's Hu Jia,
who had won the 10m gold in Athens in 2004. It felt strange to see the

people in the flesh that I had studied on TV. I thought everyone looked really different to how I imagined they would do. I was so pumped and scored 9.5s in five of the six dives in the prelim round and qualified second behind Hu by just seven points with a score of 480.050, my best score to date.

In the semis, I continued to put in a strong performance and came second again. In the finals, I fought it out for the bronze medals with the Ukrainian Konstantin Milyaev, who overtook me on the last two dives. China's Yang Liguang won the gold with 514.150 ahead of Hu, who got the silver with 510.250. In the end, I was just six points off a medal with 419.70 but I was still over the moon with my performance. Being on the big stage just didn't faze me; it just excited me and made me perform even better. I loved the buzz of it.

From each event I took something important away. After that event, I started to work with the sports psychologist to try and reverse my scores, so rather than getting 480 in the prelims, 465 in the semis and 420 in the finals, I did it the opposite way round and my scores went up. I had never competed in three rounds before and wasn't used to doing that many dives in a day, so I learned I needed to pace myself and keep my energy levels high.

As I started to go away more, it meant I was missing school, which at the time I thought was really cool. That was until I got back to school and realized all the work I needed to do. I did have to catch up so tried to do as much when I was away as I could.

In July, Callum and I competed at the ASA National Diving Championships, our first Senior National competition together, at Sheffield's Pond's Forge. We took an early lead by gaining the first 9s of the competition and for our third dive, the reverse two and a half somersaults with tuck, we achieved our highest mark of 9.5. We performed consistently throughout the final and finished on the top spot with a score of 388.38 points. Everything had gone to plan and it felt great. We had really enjoyed ourselves and knew there was room for improvement. We were looking forward to building on our performance.

THE FOLLOWING DAY WAS THE INDIVIDUAL EVENT AND I EASILY QUALIFIED FOR THE SEMI-FINALS AFTER GETTING MY FIRST 10 OF THE COMPETITION WITH MY REVERSE TWO AND A HALF SOMERSAULTS WITH TUCK, AND IN THE SEMIS TOOK THE TOP SPOT WITH 456.45 POINTS.

In the final I was up against Southampton's Blake Aldridge and Gareth Jones, who took an early lead over me. But going into the third round I hit my reverse two and a half somersaults hard and secured two 10s to take the lead. After gaining good scores in my final two dives, I took the National title with 444.20 points and became the youngest person to win the event for fifty-one years. It felt like a massive achievement and I was really proud of myself.

I was back at Pond's Forge again in September for the final leg of the FINA Series that year. At that stage I wasn't doing every single competition because my team manager was still pacing my performances, but after Pete was forced to withdraw due to injury, I was to dive in his place. It felt pretty daunting going into the competition because I was facing what looked likely to be the Olympic line-up for Beijing – it was packed with world champions. I just focused on what I had to do and put all my efforts into it. I was slightly disappointed after dropping a couple of my dives and in the end I came fourth with 441.25, agonizingly close to Russia's Gleb Galperin, who took the third podium place with 446.55 points. China's Lin Yue and Zhou Luxin won the gold and silver medals with 534.90 and 505.95, respectively.

In the synchro competition Callum and I earned GB a respectable fifth-placed finish with a personal best of 388.89. Again, the Chinese topped the podium with a score of 485.64. It was a fun day and we really enjoyed being in front of a home crowd, who are always incredibly supportive.

One day towards the end of the year, as I came through the gates after a normal day at school and climbed into the car, Dad gave me an exercise book. He had a funny smirk on his face. I opened it and on the first page it said 'Wayne Rooney', then 'Theo Walcott' on the next, 'Andy Murray' and then, on the next page, 'Tom Daley'. 'You'. I turned over. 'Have'. 'Been'. 'Nominated'. 'For The Young Sports Personality Of The Year'.

'THAT'S PRETTY COOL,' I SAID.

'KEEP TURNING,' DAD SAID, A TEAR LEAKING FROM HIS EYE.

TURNING TO THE FINAL PAGE, I READ: 'AND YOU HAVE WON.'

Dad was blubbing full on then! It felt amazing but I had to keep it a secret because I was due to go away to Montreal in Canada for the

COMPETING IN
CANADA WITH BLAKE.

CAMO invitational meet, so I filmed a video link to say thank you for the award and how honoured I felt.

In Canada, I channelled my pride into the competition and in the individual event, drawing a succession of five perfect 10s, I eventually finished sixth with 451.90. In the synchro later that day, I was diving with my new partner, Blake Aldridge. Steve Foley had put us together to see how we dived but we hadn't done any preparation. It seemed the combination was a winner, though, as we picked up our first gold medal with 440.10 points. We scored a run of 9s, 9.5s and 10s, beating Pete and Leon, who faltered on the fourth and fifth dives, finishing in second place with 432.99. I was gutted about missing the Sports Personality of the Year ceremony but everyone made a fuss of me and when I went back to school they had made a banner to say well done.

I never really spoke about my sport at school; I just tried to be normal. My mates did football and rugby and none of them came to see me dive or anything like that. But lots of people knew of my success because of my being in the papers. I think they all thought I made loads of money, but obviously that is not the case in most Olympic sports. They always saw each other more outside school than I could manage, but I did go to the cinema and bowling some weekends and I never felt like I was missing out.

At the start of the New Year, 2008, I competed at the British National Championships in Manchester Aquatics Centre. Virtually the whole family came – Mum, Dad, William and Ben, both sets of grandparents, some aunts, uncles and about five cousins. Seeing the people I love did then, and always does, drive me to do well. It also felt good to try and prove myself on home soil.

In the individual event I was trailing at the midway point and knew I needed to pull something special out of the bag to get into the top two.

By my final dive, I needed almost perfect scores to win. I managed one of the best dives I had ever done, coming away with 9s, but still didn't think I could beat Pete, who was in the lead by quite a few points.

But Pete dropped his last dive for 5s and 6s, meaning that I had won with 471.70 to his score of 462.60. It felt brilliant and everyone was over the moon for me. There's a video of Dad somewhere upstairs and you can hear him letting out a succession of small gulps and then a giant sob as he realized I had beaten Pete to the title.

HE KEPT SAYING, 'HE'S THE BRITISH CHAMPION! YOU ALWAYS SEE SPORTS FANS FOLLOWING OTHER PEOPLE AROUND, NOW THEY ARE FOLLOWING MY SON AROUND – COOL!'

In the synchro event Leon and Pete had withdrawn because Leon had a hernia so Blake and I automatically qualified to go to the World Cup in July to try out for the Olympics, which was brilliant. We continued to dive consistently, matching each other's form in the air, and won the event with 431.25 points. Our best round, the fifth, saw us score over 90 for our backward three and a half somersaults with tuck.

Later in January, we went back to Madrid for another FINA World Series event and in the synchro we were up against some of the best pairings in the world, including the Chinese, Germans, Russians and Canadians. Blake and I continued to perform well and secured a silver medal with 417.93 points. It wasn't the best we had performed, but we were getting good marks for synchronization and did a really good inward three and a half tuck. We really felt as if we were pushing the Chinese pair, Yang Liguang and Hao Zhang, and even though we didn't catch them, they knew we were close and we scored above 400, which was our aim. At that point, despite the huge age difference – Blake was twenty-five and I was only thirteen, our relationship was really good. I looked up to him as an older brother or uncle figure and we got on well at first.

The next day, with the Chinese divers Hu Jia and Yang Liguang ahead, Pete and I fought it out for bronze in the individual competition. I was determined to stay close to the Chinese and even scored four perfect 10s on my first dive. After Pete dropped his back two and a half somersaults and two and a half twists, the way was clear for me to overtake him and I performed a good back three and a half tuck. I was still on a very low degree of difficulty then so got 9s and 9.5s all the way through, finishing on a final score of 495.45. Yang Liguang got silver with 506.55 and Hu won gold on 540.75.

Most dives take about three months to learn, but after that event Andy taught me one dive in three days. I was only using the reverse two and a half tuck at that point and one day he suggested I have a go off 5m and then he told me that we'd learn the reverse three and a half off 10m. In the next three days we did all the somersaults on the land, then in the rig on the land and then in the rig in the pool, and by day three I was doing it off 10m like I'd been doing it for months. The feeling when you do a new dive is amazing because you never know what it's going to be like. When you hit the water it's such a relief and you immediately want to do it again to ingrain it into your head.

That year it was competitions back to back and I was starting to get used to being away and felt less and less homesick every time.

BY MY FINAL DIVE, I NEEDED
ALMOST PERFECT SCORES TO WIN.
I MANAGED ONE OF THE BEST DIVES
I HAD EVER DONE, COMING AWAY
WITH 9S, BUT STILL DIDN'T THINK
I COULD BEAT PETE, WHO WAS IN
THE LEAD BY QUITE A FEW POINTS.

I always called home regularly and had my laptop with me so I could speak to my friends on Facebook. Being away was feeling more and more like an adventure. In February, it was on to Beijing for the FINA World Cup and Olympics qualifier. A field of over 300 divers were competing for 136 places at the summer's Games. I, like all the other divers from team GB, had a lot of expectation on my shoulders but I had no fear, I just felt really relaxed and enthusiastic about the event. It was the longest time away from home though, as I was going for almost four weeks, but my homesickness was getting better by then and I normally only felt wobbly for a day or two.

DAD HAD DECIDED TO COME OUT TO THE EVENT ON HIS OWN WITHOUT A GUARANTEE OF ACTUALLY SEEING ME BECAUSE HE HAD NOT BEEN ABLE TO GET A TICKET AND WAS RELYING ON BUYING ONE FROM A TOUT – HE MANAGED TO GET ONE FOR THREE TIMES THE FACE VALUE.

Thinking about it now, he was really brave to come out on his own. He always came everywhere. Mum helped me pack my clothes, as always, and after my previous food experiences in China I was a bit worried, so made sure I packed some emergency Pot Noodles, just in case.

The Chinese are like machines. They work so hard and are pushed by their coaches. It doesn't matter if they are injured because they have other people who can dive just as well. They go to year-round boot-camp-style training designed to produce gold medals around the world and most of them spend very little time on their school work; it is all about their sport. They have dominated the sport, particularly the women, for a long time. Fu Mingxia, for example, is probably the most famous female Chinese diver after winning four Olympic gold medals in diving, two for 10m individual and two for 3m springboard.

She went to a Beijing Sports School when she was nine and trained for seven hours a day, six days a week. She only saw her parents once a year. When the Chinese are younger, their parents make the decision whether they want them to be musicians, well educated or sportsmen or sportswomen and they keep working at it for their whole life. The diving training sounds brutal. The Chinese coaches are very forceful but are normally technically excellent. It's a very different culture; one that I'm sure I would do really badly in.

When we arrived in Beijing, some of the other GB divers – Tonia, Blake, Stacie Powell and Ben Swain – and I managed to sneak into the Water Cube. There wasn't much security so we crept into the complex and just kept going until we reached the pool area. I was blown away. It was amazing and I kept thinking, 'This is what the Olympic pool is going to look like.' It was really futuristic and brightly coloured – like something out of Mario Brothers. The walls were inflatable so you could squeeze them in and they would pop back out again. There were 18,000 seats, which is the largest number of people I would ever have dived in front of. We all managed to rush up to the 10m boards and take each other's pictures before a security guard saw us and chased us away!

On the fourth day, Blake and I stepped forward for the synchro event. There was a lot riding on it because we needed a top eight finish to guarantee the GB team a place at the Olympics. We faltered in the prelims finishing in ninth – at one stage thinking we might not make it – but were more confident in the final and everything seemed to come together for us. The Chinese audience, who regard diving as a national treasure, really got behind us. Our first dive, a forward one and a half somersaults in piked position, earned us 9.5s and we dived consistently from then. The Chinese pair were out front from the very first dive and took the gold with 482.46, Germany collected the silver with 466.74 and we took the bronze with 446.07. Blake and I were thrilled. It really felt like all our hard work had been rewarded. However, it was still no guarantee we would make the Olympics because while we had assured Great Britain a place, we were still due to face Pete and Leon in June for the decider.

The following day was the individual event. In the semi-finals, Pete finished fourth out of eighteen while I was ninth. The Chinese were cheering almost as much for me as they were for their own divers, which gave me a boost. In the finals I scored 9s for my opening dive – a back two and a half somersaults, one and a half twists, to place second in round two. I then earned 8.5s for my forward three and a half. By halfway through, I was fourth with my most difficult dives to come. I was always going to be at a disadvantage as my tariffs were lower than those of the other competitors. And with the pressure mounting, I missed my armstand back triple and plummeted down the rankings. I knew I needed to stay upbeat – and did a solid back three and a half. For my final dive, a reverse three and a half, I was standing on the edge thinking I just had to go for it. I remember it being a great takeoff, squeezing into my tuck shape, slow spinning and kicking out perfectly, and I was rewarded by the judges with four 10s. I came seventh with 480.40.

TO KNOW I WAS GOING TO THE OLYMPICS WAS UNBELIEVABLE. I DON'T THINK IT REALLY SANK IN FOR A FEW DAYS. I FELT TOTALLY FLOORED, THAT I WOULD BE FULFILLING SOMETHING I HAD DREAMT ABOUT SO HARD.

I was hollering, 'I'm going to the Olympics!' Dad was crying, obviously.

I was hugging everyone in the team. Afterwards there was a press conference. Diving in China is like football is in England and they are obsessed with it. Blake and I, two Germans and two Chinese were sat at the front and every single question was directed towards me. I felt quite awkward but answered everyone's questions the best I could.

Cameras were flashing, videos cameras were pointing at me, the crowd were cheering wildly. I loved it. Dave Richards, who was dealing with the GB team's media, Dad and Andy were all simultaneously fielding requests by the media on their phones – it just went mental.

On my return to the UK, it was just as crazy. I did interviews for the BBC, Radio 1, the *Daily Mail* and *The Times*, among others. Everyone was calling me 'Dynamic Daley' and 'Baby Daley' a 'pocket-sized phenomenon'. They just asked me about how I was feeling – I could have talked for weeks. My family had a bit of a gathering for me to celebrate and there were journalists knocking at the door and satellite vans outside the house. Mum and Dad were enjoying the attention, too. I wanted to do every interview I was offered because doing so much national press was relatively new.

After four weeks away I was exhausted but was anxious to catch up with my friends. School was really good. They were still giving me work to go away with and were helping me catch up. My friends were really normal and I slotted back as if I hadn't been away. It could never go to my head because my family and friends just treated me exactly the same.

IT KIND OF BYPASSED ME THAT THE MEDIA WERE REPORTING THAT I WAS THE YOUNGEST PERSON TO EVER GO TO THE OLYMPICS.

I think about it like this – I was young, of course, but I was still diving alongside everyone else. A couple of days later, Kenneth Lester came out saying he was the youngest by a couple of months. I would be 14 years and 81 days at the start of the Games in August, while Lester was aged 13 years and 144 days when he competed in Rome as part of the Great Britain rowing squad in 1960, but his date of birth had been recorded wrongly on the British Olympic Association database. All the media changed their reports but I didn't mind – all I cared about was that I was going to the Olympics.

The *Sunday Times* arranged for Kenneth to come down to Plymouth from his home in Oxfordshire to meet a few days later and he passed on his experience of the Olympics. He told me: 'Enjoy every minute of it and remember as much as you can.'

He also said he was reluctant to take the limelight away from me but I didn't mind. I tried on his blazer with the Union Jack and Rome 1960 stitched on the pocket – it fitted pretty well. He said he was 6st 12lb when he was there and had to put a sandbag in the boat to make up the right weight, I was around seven and a half stone then. I also leafed though the programmes from his event and saw the letters he had written to his parents and brother. It's weird to think of him not being able to call home or text and email. He told me to keep a diary so I could look back at it, which I did. Later he and his wife, Ros, watched me dive, but because of the jetlag I stuck to the lower boards.

I was definitely starting to get recognized more and more. I remember walking through town one day with my Aunty Marie and people started asking for photos and autographs. It felt like a real novelty. It was so weird to think that in a few months I would be able to call myself an Olympian.

'I REMEMBER, ON ONE DAY, ALL THESE
CAMERAS WERE PRECARIOUSLY POSED
ON THE DIFFERENT DIVING BOARDS AT
THE MAYFLOWER, ALL TRYING TO GET
THE BEST SHOTS OF ME LEAPING FROM
THE 10M BOARD. IT WAS SURREAL.'

IN THE
PUBLIC
EYE

In March the GB team travelled to Eindhoven for the European Diving Championships, so I was only back home for a few weeks. Blake and I really wanted another medal – by that point we were ranked second in the world.

I DIVED WELL BUT BLAKE WASN'T QUITE THERE AND MISSED A COUPLE. WE ENDED UP COMING FIFTH. I WASN'T FRUSTRATED WITH HIM BUT IT WAS ANNOYING BECAUSE I FELT I'D DIVED REALLY WELL, SO THERE WAS NOTHING I COULD DO ABOUT IT.

But you always take it as a team because that's the nature of synchro. I didn't want to go to the mixed zone where the world's media were waiting, because it felt like everything had gone wrong, but once we got in there it was OK, because we were able to explain what had happened.

After our event the team manager called the whole diving team together for a meeting. He was angry because he felt the team were not diving to the best of their ability and we weren't making the finals. There was only my event left and, going into the individual, I wanted to show people what I could do. I was diving against Germany's Sascha Klein and the World Champion Gleb Galperin, as well as Dmitriy Dobroskok of Russia and Ukraine's Konstantin Milyaev. It was a pretty tough field so I wasn't expecting a medal.

I went into round two placed second after my backward two and a half somersaults, one and a half twists, and kept pace with the leaders with a good forward three and a half piked, but I missed my entry on the inward three and a half with tuck, and a low score of 59.20 saw me slip to sixth with a score of 222. I thought I had just thrown a medal away – but it wasn't just me who was having a hard time, thankfully. Sascha missed two dives in a row and Gleb was returning from injury, so he was struggling too. My armstand triple somersaults with tuck gave me four 10s from the judges and my fifth dive, a backward three and a half with tuck, got another four 10s! It wasn't my best dive but I did enough with my reverse three and a half with tuck, to give me a total of 491.95 to win my first senior international title. Sascha took silver with a score of 487.60 and Italy's Francesco Dell'Uomo took the bronze with 481.30. It was days like those that I had always dreamt about. My performance wasn't the best but I held it together and in the end it was enough. It feels so hard to explain what it meant to me and how happy I was. I didn't know what to do with myself. I thought back to the times I said I would never go back onto 10m and felt so relieved I had made it back up there.

Mum, Dad, my brothers and grandparents were all watching, and as soon as I won Dad was on the phone to the rest of the family. When he called my Uncle Jamie – who we sometimes call Jamie Junglebeans – he said, 'Tom Daley is European Champion,' and my uncle thought he was kidding!

Again the media hype went into overdrive. Some of the people who had not picked up on what happened at the World Cup started to talk about how I could be a medal hope in Beijing. Some days it felt like a constant round of TV and newspaper interviews. I remember, on one day, all these cameras were precariously posed on the different diving boards at the Mayflower, all trying to get the best shots of me leaping from the 10m board. It was surreal. We soon realized that I was spending so much time doing interviews that we needed to pass all handling of the media side to my agent so they could control it better and I still had enough time to train properly, go to school and do my homework. But I loved the interviews; I had never found myself nervous or shy.

One day, I did a photoshoot at the end of Plymouth Leander
Swimming Club's old diving platform, going into the sea in
my Speedos, and it was freezing.

I WAS QUICKLY REALIZING THAT I SEEMED TO BE MORE RECOGNIZABLE WITHOUT ANY CLOTHES ON. IT DIDN'T BOTHER ME – IT'S WHAT I WAS USED TOO!

I went back to school as normal. My best friends, Sophie, Nikita, Harriet
and Alex, just treated me as they always had done. Nikita was my first
girlfriend and we went out for a few weeks when I was thirteen. We
held hands and stuff but it fizzled out. We have remained great mates.
But other people at school chose to single me out and call me 'Diver
Boy'. It didn't worry me; I knew what I had achieved and was proud of

myself. Then, when some of the older boys started calling me 'Speedo Boy', I thought it was an amusing nickname. I let them get on with it and ignored it. Little did I know that there would be worse to come.

Three days after my fourteenth birthday I was back competing in Sheffield for the second leg of the FINA World Diving Series. In the synchro Blake and I put in the best performance we had done until then and, after scoring our first perfect 10 of the series, we picked up the first British gold of the series with 429.12 points.

In the individual event I made it comfortably into the semis and, after only making a couple of mistakes, into the final. I started strongly, scoring 9s for my first dive, but then over-rotated my inward three and a half somersaults and slipped back slightly. Halfway through I was in second place, but in the fourth round Pete did a great back three and a half somersaults, to score all 9s from the judges, and moved up into second place. But I fought my way back into the silver medal position, ripping my back three and a half somersaults. In the end, I took silver with 473.15, just 0.2 points ahead of Pete with China's Huo Liang in the top spot with 518.4.

Just a couple of days later, I boarded the plane for Nanjing, for the final round of the FINA Series. Dad and my Granddad Dink were watching. Annoyingly, I lost the silver medal in the individual event after messing up my final dive, my reverse three and a half, and finished fourth with 474.55 with Zhou Luxin winning with a phenomenal score 581.60. That is the only time I have ever dropped that dive to make me fall back down the rankings. The Chinese led the whole event and took eight gold medals across all the competitions. I was a bit frustrated but tried to take something away from the event. Each of the events was just about learning and tweaking as I went along, to try and put in the best performance possible.

IN MY SPEEDOS POSING ON
PLYMOUTH HOE – IT WAS SOOO COLD!

Around then Leon announced his retirement after taking advice from the doctors about a persistent back injury that he was told was untreatable, so we would not face him and Pete in the dive-off the following month in Manchester, and Blake and I were definitely going to compete at the Olympics together, which made me doubly excited. Leon would still come as a commentator and mentor for the team.

In June, Mum, Dad and I went to Number 10 Downing Street to meet the Prime Minister at the time, Gordon Brown. It was the launch of the Government initiative whereby the under-16s and over-60s could go swimming in their local pools. I thought it was a great idea as I take being active for granted, but I know some people do not have access to the kind of swimming facilities that I do. I wanted to use my new-found fame to help people. There is no point sitting at home and doing nothing. If you can help someone you do, and if what you do helps just one person, it makes a difference.

NUMBER 10 FELT LIKE SOME SORT OF TARDIS. FROM THE OUTSIDE, IT LOOKED LIKE A SMALL RECTANGULAR HOUSE, BUT ONCE WE GOT INSIDE THE DOOR, IT BRANCHED INTO FOUR HOUSES – IT WAS HUGE.

We were taken into a room where there were some media and people were handing out orange juice and croissants. Gordon Brown came over and we chatted about the Olympics and my training. I didn't feel uncomfortable because he was really normal, and told my parents they had done a good job with me, which they were pleased about.

Six days later I was back in London to launch the GB kit for the Olympics. Each year they do a PR stunt to show the public how the kit looks for that year. Some of the other athletes, like Victoria Pendleton,

Chris Tomlinson, Liz Fell and I wore various bits of kit and stood in the window of the Adidas shop on Oxford Street. I didn't wear my Speedos because they thought it might be a bit inappropriate, so I just wore a tracksuit. Dad came and took photos. We were like mannequins behind the glass and had to try to stay really still, and we got some pretty strange looks from members of the public.

But the next day I saw even more media as I attended a press day in Plymouth. It was a full and intense day of interviews and there were camera crews from all over the world, including Japan and America. Everyone wanted to know about my plans for the next few months and what I was aiming for.

Then, after a busy few days working, I really enjoyed celebrating my Dad's birthday. We had a big party at my Grandma Rose's house with a marquee. It was nice to have a break from all the intense media attention and enjoy spending some time with my family.

I didn't get much of a rest, though, as about a week later I travelled up north with the rest of the team to a training camp in Leeds and then the Olympic qualifiers. I had three days of training with Blake, working on our list. It was good to get some consistent training together with only a month until we took part in the biggest competition in the world. I was starting to enjoy being away with everyone more and more and the diving team was becoming my family away from my family. We always try and make our time away from home as much fun as possible.

THE DAY BEFORE THE SYNCHRO COMPETITION, BLAKE FELL OFF HIS MOTORBIKE AND HURT HIS ARM, SO WE WERE NOT ABLE TO COMPETE TOGETHER, BUT IN MY INDIVIDUAL I BROKE THROUGH THE 500-POINT BARRIER FOR THE FIRST TIME WITH 512 POINTS.

Although my place had already been confirmed, the team was named and there was an increasing sense of excitement about Beijing. I still could not believe I was going, but to finally know that my hard work had paid off felt amazing and I was determined to enjoy every second of my Olympic experience. The other names confirmed as part of the GB Diving Team were Tonia, Pete, Blake, Ben Swain and Nick Robinson-Baker, Hayley Sage, Tandi Gerrard, Stacie Powell and Rebecca Gallantree.

I went on holiday with my family to Alcudia in Majorca for a week of relaxation, just being a normal family, playing together in the pool and on the beach and going out for dinner in the evenings. Mum and Dad always tried to give us all a break, despite the financial pressure. I loved the time we had just as a family but when we came back I was hungrier than ever for the Olympics. A week without diving made me realize how much it means to me and I still feel the same when I go away now.

Me and my brothers. Messing around with special effects definitely had a 'special effect' on Ben . . .

In the run-up to Beijing, I was training six or seven times a week for about three or four hours at a time. Everything was focused towards the event and perfecting my list. I didn't think about the pressure. It was just about going to have the experience. I still potentially had four Olympics so wanted to learn as much from it as I could. As well as dry board and diving sessions, I had massage once a week to loosen up my muscles. It's not a soft tissue massage; it's really deep so they go at you with their elbows, which can be quite painful but it definitely helps the next day. I also had physio once a week to stretch me out or if I needed extra specific work on an area. Some days Dad would take me to the pool, sometimes three to four times a day. On a Friday, for example, I would get to school for 8.30 a.m. for one lesson, then go training in the pool, then go back to school for another lesson, then go back to the pool for a massage, then school, then home for some food and to do my homework and then get back to the pool by 5.30 p.m. for three hours' more training.

IT WAS ABOUT THAT TIME THAT I STARTED TO BE DRUGS TESTED AND TWO PEOPLE WOULD JUST TURN UP AT THE DOOR WITH NO WARNING AND I WOULD HAVE TO PEE INTO A CUP. IT WAS SLIGHTLY ODD THE FIRST FEW TIMES – THEY ALSO WATCH! – BUT NOW I'M USED TO IT.

July got off to a good start when I travelled up to the NEC in Birmingham to pick up my GB Olympics kit. There were personal shoppers everywhere and we got measured up and could take anything we wanted. Tonia and I were together and we were running round, trying loads of things on. I picked up some T-shirts, shorts and, of course, my trunks. Each of us had to get a formal suit, parade wear, a pillow and a Panasonic camcorder. It really started to sink in that I was actually going and there were so many people there that it made me feel like I was part of a bigger team.

The following week, Tonia and I had a really busy week. We were going round schools in the town, talking in assemblies to advertise free diving lessons to encourage more people to try the sport. All the children put their hands up for leaflets and said they wanted to start diving, which was good. We did two assemblies a day for five days and had training and schoolwork on top of that. I also had lunch with Sir Steve Redgrave. Steve watched me training from the spectator gallery at

Central Park pool and it felt quite weird that he was there. Each time the receptionists see TV cameras, they get the signing-in book ready, hoping that it might be someone famous. Over lunch at a restaurant on Plymouth Hoe, Steve and I chatted about the Olympics and what to expect. Each time I saw him, I always asked him about dealing with nerves and he encouraged me to stay focused and keep working hard.

That week I had another exciting day for a different reason – I had my braces taken off! Initially I had a removable brace and then train tracks for about eighteen months. At first, I thought they were cool but about two days later I wanted to get them off again! I got food stuck in them, and they hurt, so I was determined have them taken off before the Olympics. The following day I went to Frankie and Benny's with my friends as a bit of a send-off for me going to Beijing. We also had the family over and it gave me a chance to say goodbye to everyone.

The following week, I was with the British Diving Team at a training camp in Sheffield. We had lunch and a talk from Steve Foley. He said lots of thank yous to everyone and it was a big morale booster for the team. In the evening we went bowling and played athletes versus the coaches. We won the first game but the coaches beat us in the second. It was really nice to spend some time with the other divers, especially Tonia and Ben. The next day we went for a really posh meal to mark us going to the Olympics.

I DIDN'T HAVE THE RIGHT CLOTHES. I ONLY HAD A T-SHIRT, JEANS AND TRAINERS AND £20 IN MY POCKET. BUT TONIA CONSIDERED IT A CHALLENGE AND TOOK ME TO PRIMARK, WHERE I GOT SMART SHOES, SHIRT AND TROUSERS FOR UNDER £20. WE WERE LIKE BOOM – DONE!

There was still a lot of media attention on me prior to us heading out to Beijing, and Steve Foley went on *BBC Radio 5 Live* to say that if it wasn't all properly managed for me, there was a definite danger of me burning out. I could understand why he was saying it but I didn't feel like there was any problem. I had such a good team looking after me, great support from my family, a new agent, the British federation's media officer, who was very supportive, and people like Steve around me all the time. I think if any of them thought it was all getting too much, they would have told me.

Despite the huge interest, bizarrely I didn't feel any greater stress than normal because I didn't think I was going to get a medal. I knew there was always a chance but I never expected it. Andy always says there's a chance and 'If my aunty had balls, she'd be my uncle', so there is no point thinking 'what if'. I still think there was greater pressure going to China earlier in the year for the World Cup. My goal was to get above 500 as I had only ever done that once before in a competition. My programme was exactly the same one that I used in the World Cup, so I would be using all the same dives. I wanted to come home feeling proud of myself. That obviously brings pressure but it is a demand I have to handle in every competition, so I felt fine about it. I knew my best chance of a place was in the synchro. The prelim of that was the World Cup, so Blake and I knew we were in the final and there were only eight pairs competing. Anything can happen there. The Greek pair only got into the event in 2004 because the Games were in Athens and they ended up winning because others didn't dive well, so anything can happen on the day. The individual platform is different because I had to make it through two rounds before even getting to the final. My attitude going to the Games was that it was all about the experience – and to do a good performance. Anything more than that would just be a bonus and I could not wait.

THE 2008 OLYMPICS

I woke up bright and early on 27 July – the day I was to leave for Beijing. It was a normal morning with Mum shouting at me to come and get my breakfast and as I legged it downstairs the whole family shouted, 'Morning, Tom!' I think they had been planning it. Dad was videoing as I ate my Nesquik cereal. Putting my Olympic tracksuit on for real felt very surreal. I snapped shut my suitcase, forgetting my Nintendo Wii.

After leaving, and going back to pick up the Wii, we met Andy and Tonia and there was a group of people to wave us off, including our families and Tonia's boyfriend. I said goodbye to my family. Ben was hanging off my neck and William gave me a rare hug.

In the car, Tonia and I unwrapped a present from Brooke, which she insisted that we opened on the way to the airport. Brooke had sadly missed getting a place by an agonizing five points. She got me a SpongeBob SquarePants keyring and Tonia a Patrick Star one to put on our GB bags. We attached them – and sent her a picture to let her know we had opened them. Everywhere we stopped on our journey, we were recognized and I signed loads of autographs. Everyone was wishing us luck.

On the flight we amused ourselves with the mini ping-pong table belonging to one of the 3m synchro divers, Ben Swain, eating Haribo and trying unsuccessfully to get upgraded. I had mentioned Haribo in an interview, saying I loved their sweets, so they sent loads to the house, which was great.

Arriving in Beijing, there was a complete media scrum – the cameras were flashing and I felt like one of those famous Hollywood stars. I wasn't allowed to do any interviews until after my competition so had to ignore most of them. Stepping outside, it was so humid, like being

in a giant steam room. The journey to the Olympic village was only about forty-five minutes and we even had our own Olympic lane! Everywhere in Beijing there were tall buildings, giant cinemas and 24-hour cafés.

THE SIZE OF THE OLYMPIC VILLAGE WAS MIND-BLOWING – IT WAS LIKE A MINI CITY. THE FOOD HALL WAS THE SIZE OF FOUR FOOTBALL PITCHES WITH DISHES FROM COUNTRIES ALL AROUND THE WORLD AND YOU COULD GET AS MUCH AS YOU WANTED, WHENEVER YOU WANTED.

There was a post office where you could send postcards home with a picture of yourself on the stamp, a cinema, huge gym, outdoor pool, a hairdresser's, shops and a games room with arcade games.

The bedrooms were like very basic student accommodation. In a way it was better, because we could make them feel more homely and stick up our Good Luck cards around the wall and put posters up. It's traditional for synchro partners to share rooms and to go to bed and get up at the same time, so I shared with Blake. He was a good roommate and I know he liked my positive attitude. While he was twelve years older than me, we clicked when we dived together and felt like we were sharing an incredible journey.

There was a whole team of people with us: Steve Foley, the team manager; the national performance director, Kim White; the coaches, including Andy; the physios, psychologists and doctors. In GB HQ, there were media coordinators, people who sorted the tickets, staff who looked after the accommodation – the list was endless.

The psychologists were there to help us be as positive as we could. They talked us through the 'What if?' situations: What if I split my trunks on the first dive? You have to make sure you have an extra pair of trunks in your bag. What if I lose my chamois? Take an extra chamois. What if there is bad news at home? Would you want to know or not? You have to sort out things like that before you go, so you are totally carefree and can focus entirely on the task in hand.

For three days we trained at the Water Cube, which went really well. The rest of the time we explored the village and on one afternoon I went to the market and bought some Chanel bags for my friends, Harriet and Sophie. Everything was so bright and colourful. The local area had an amazing feel to it – the people really got behind all the athletes, no matter what sport or country we were from. Everyone respected you. If they saw you wearing a tracksuit they would want pictures, autographs and the chance to shake your hand. It really was overwhelming. I managed to keep in touch with my friends and family on my laptop. I also sent Team GB postcards home.

We then travelled to Xian for a five-day training camp. We went there because it's one of China's regional diving centres, a brilliant place where there is everything we need to prepare. There is an amazing dry-land area with huge trampolines, overhead rigging, a

foam pit and crash mats. It was perfect for the run-up to the big competition.

We stayed at the Shangri-La Hotel and it was like living in luxury. The rooms were incredible with huge comfy beds and massive bathrooms and they had floor-to-ceiling windows, so the views over the city were pretty spectacular. It was there that we were first told about an article in the *Daily Mail* about Tonia and me, and how well we got on. The other athletes called Tonia, Ben and me the 'Sunshine Group' because we were always so happy when we were together. I know there were loads of stories in the Beijing press about Tonia and me being together, and everyone kept asking if she was my girlfriend. Nowadays she's just like a sister, but on that trip she was more of a mother, looking after me! In all her press conferences they would always ask her and she would say no, but on the odd occasion she would say yes to see their reactions!

Our time in Xian revolved around dry-land and pool training and meetings. My diving was really consistent and I felt very calm and happy. We often watched our session played back on video to see where we could improve, which was helpful.

We also staged competitions as if they were for real with a parade, scores and announcements, and spoke to the nutritionist about food on our competition days.

In my downtime I mainly played on my Wii and watched videos with Tonia, which helped me relax. I didn't really socialize with Blake, who mainly stuck with Pete and the older divers. In Xian itself, it was fairly boring, but there was a Starbucks so we always stopped for Frappucinos. We did go to a drive-in golf range, which was amusing because Andy broke a club when he let it go and it snapped against the ceiling, and I managed to hit the man driving a tractor who picked up all the balls.

AT OUR FINAL TEAM MEETING BEFORE HEADING BACK TO BEIJING, WE WERE GIVEN GIANT FLAGS AND BLOW-UP UNION JACK HANDS. I FELT REALLY EXCITED BUT WAS ALSO STRANGELY SAD TO SAY GOODBYE TO XIAN AND EVERYONE WHO HAD BEEN HELPING US THERE, AS IT ALREADY FELT LIKE THAT PART OF OUR OLYMPIC JOURNEY WAS OVER.

We arrived back in Beijing on 5 August and going back to the Olympic Village was like being right back at home. Everyone had started arriving and it was good to meet or catch up with the other British athletes, like Victoria Pendleton and Beth Tweddle. I met Rafael Nadal one day and got a picture with him – everyone joked that he probably thought I was a ball boy. I teased Tonia loads, because she thought he was really good-looking. I also saw Usain Bolt in the village, but when the really famous athletes were going to the food hall, they were always surrounded by lots of people.

One day I was with Tonia and we were eating breakfast when Jamie and Andy Murray asked if they could sit with us. I almost choked on

my cereal. I could not believe they knew my name. I didn't know what to say. But we just talked about the competition. Andy comes across as a quiet and moody type on TV but he was really upbeat and talkative.

In the first week there was a function at the British Embassy, where they took team photos and there were speeches. We had nominated Pete from the diving team to be the flag bearer but the swimmer Mark Foster was given the job. Gabby Logan, Sue Barker and Jake Humphrey wished me luck and told me to have fun. I even met Princess Anne, who wasn't what I expected at all. She was really chatty and funny.

The opening ceremony held at the Beijing National Stadium – the Bird's Nest – was incredible. It all kicked off at 8 p.m. in the evening on the 8th of August – 8 is considered a lucky number to the Chinese. There was some debate about whether I should go because my competition was only a couple of days later, but Sir Steve Redgrave advised me to, saying that he thought I would recover quickly and it would be worth it for the experience and the boost it would give me, and it definitely was.

We were all waiting in this holding area, which was the gymnastics hall, for hours. Tonia and I played the card game Chase the Ace with Andy and Jamie, which helped pass the time. We were wearing our special GB suits, with blue shirts and white jackets and, after standing up for about three hours waiting to go, were all so hot and sweaty, we looked like we had been diving. When they started calling the names of the countries to get ready to line up, each time they announced another team, everyone booed! We were number 116.

WHEN WE FINALLY REACHED THE TUNNEL TO GO INTO THE STADIUM, THE NOISE WAS UNREAL, THE CROWD WAS ROARING. NOTHING COULD HAVE PREPARED ME FOR THE ASSAULT ON MY SENSES. THE STADIUM WAS SO HUGE AND PACKED. DESPITE THE FACT I WAS BOILING, I FELT GOOSE PIMPLES UP MY ARMS AND SHIVERS GOING UP MY SPINE. MY HEART WAS HAMMERING.

It felt like all the hard work was worth it and knowing I was there to represent the country was awesome. I was waving a small Union Jack and smiling to the cameras as we walked. When China came out the stadium erupted. We watched it all unfold on the big screen. There were over 2,000 drummers with glowing drumsticks, fireworks and colourful dancers. Then they lit the Olympic flame and raised the flags. It was phenomenal.

Afterwards I flopped into a bed at 2 a.m. I was exhausted but it was an experience that I will remember forever.

Training continued as normal and my parents had arrived with William and Ben and both sets of grandparents. I met them in the Team GB Lodge, a huge room for the British athletes, where you could get food and drinks or watch the BBC coverage of the games on a huge screen. I played the Beijing Olympic 2008 game on the Xbox with my brothers and when we tried the diving, it was really difficult! It was good to see everyone. They brought me a few treats from home that I had requested, including some Sherbet Dib Dabs, and some underwater cameras.

Tonia, Ben and I also enjoyed seeing the divers from the other countries. We got on really well with the American divers Tom Fincham and Mary Beth Dunnichay. We had a really good talk to them about how our diving was going and how things were at home. After we left them to go back to our apartments, Mary Beth and I exchanged a few flirty texts, which made my day!

Whenever anyone in the team was competing we would blow up our inflatable Union Jack hands and cheer them on. So the following day, after training, we cheered the girls in the 3m synchro. The British team came eighth but they dived really well and it was very close. It was the night before my synchro competition and I felt so upbeat. I just wanted to have fun and could not wait to see everyone waving their flags for Blake and me.

We went through our list of dives in the warm-up while all the other teams were warming up too, but we just focused on what were doing. Then it got serious as we put our tracksuits on and paraded around the pool. Sports minister Gerry Sutcliffe, Olympics minister Tessa Jowell and VIPs, including Bill and Melinda Gates, were on the poolside. I was buzzing with adrenalin.

The Chinese call me 'Baby Daley' and the audience were shouting 'Daley, Daley' at me and taking loads of pictures. I'm not sure why they don't call me Tom.

STANDING ON THE EDGE OF THE BOARD AND SEEING THE OLYMPIC RINGS STARING BACK AT ME FROM THE BOTTOM OF THE POOL WAS UNBELIEVABLE – I COULD NOT BELIEVE IT WAS REAL AND I WAS ACTUALLY THERE.

My heart was beating hard and I was sweating a lot so had to keep wiping my face. Our first two dives went well and we were in about fourth or fifth position. Then we did our inward three and a half and, while the synchronization

was good, we both went short. It wasn't a disaster though – we were only around fifth or sixth. We followed this with a back three and a half. Again, the synchro was OK but, while Blake did a perfect entry, I went over. We still had the more difficult dives to go, so I knew we could pull it back and it was important to focus on the positives and moving forwards.

Our fifth dive was the reverse three and a half and Blake landed on his back on the way in and that's when he started to get angry.

'For god's sake, why can't we do this?' he said.

I replied: 'Let's finish with a good one; let's show everyone we can do it.'

I put my earphones in to get back into the zone. I listen to upbeat stuff to get me pumped up.

THEN I SAW HIM ON THE PHONE. IT WAS WEIRD HE HAD HIS PHONE ON HIM FULL STOP – IT WAS THE OLYMPIC FINAL. I WAS GOING TO LET IT GO BUT I TOOK AN EARPHONE OUT TO SEE WHO HE WAS SPEAKING TO.

'I'm sorry, Mum, I don't know what's happening, and it's not going very well,' he was saying. 'Tom's being all moody.'

I called over to him.

'Blake, shouldn't you be off your phone now? Don't apologize to your mum. We need to go out there and show everyone what we can do.'

'Don't tell me what to do. I can do what I want.'

That's when I looked at him and put my earphones back in. I felt really annoyed and thought, 'Just grow up, Blake!'

In the end he walked up for our final dive – the back two and a half somersaults with one and a half twists – with a defeated expression and his chamois cloth around his neck. It was a good effort but wasn't enough to push us up the board. We finished with a total of 408.48 in eighth place. The Chinese who won gold were 60 points ahead of us with 468.18. It was disappointing but I didn't feel awful; I knew we could have done better but I was determined to learn from the experience.

The only reason that it got into the press was because we were walking into the mixed zone where all the cameras were with Dave Richards, the media guy. The Chinese press were first in the line and were asking me lots of questions, under the dazzling TV lights. I was telling them how it went, trying to be as positive as possible.

'YEAH, OF COURSE WE ARE DISAPPOINTED BUT IT WAS A GREAT EXPERIENCE AND I REALLY ENJOYED MYSELF. I HAD SO MUCH FUN OUT THERE. THAT'S ALL YOU CAN ASK, GETTING THE EXPERIENCE. NOW I'M LOOKING TO 2012, LIKE I'VE ALWAYS SAID . . . '

The English media were separate and, while I was still talking, they beckoned Blake over. He sneaked off and we didn't think anything of it. I guess they had spotted our body language on the poolside. By the time we got nearer to him, I could hear him.

'I wasn't on the top of my game, but I out-dived Thomas and that's not something that normally happens. He was very nervous, more so than ever before. He had a pop at me before the last dive, when we were sitting down. I saw my mum in the audience and asked her to give me a call and he said, "Why are you on the phone? We're still in the competition and we've got another dive to do." That's just Thomas – he's over-nervous. Thomas should not be worrying about what I'm doing, but he was worrying about everyone and everything and that's the sole reason he didn't perform.'

Dave Richards was soon in there, pushing him away.

'That's enough now. No more press. We're leaving,' he said.

Obviously I was annoyed but I didn't really think we'd had a big falling out. We were sharing a room after all.

I went back to the GB Lodge where my family were with Blake and it was just normal with us. Mum and Dad congratulated us both and I got lots of hugs from everyone. I played on the Xbox with my brothers and then back in our accommodation that evening, I played Cow Racing with the diver Ben Swain on my Wii to unwind.

The next day it was all over the papers. Blake was clearly really embarrassed. He said, 'You need to tell them what I said and that's not what I think. It's ruined my image.'

I said to him, 'You're the one who said it. They've quoted you. You're the one that needs to get yourself out of the mess.'

We still didn't know the scale of it in the UK. It's like being in the Big Brother house in the village; you do not know anything about what's going on outside. Dad had been given the heads-up by some of the journalists that he had got to know at competitions and he was particularly furious about it.

He thought it wasn't exactly good team spirit and each time I tried to bat it away saying it wasn't serious, he disagreed. He was right. I felt quite let down and a bit deflated. It was awkward then. We did an interview together to try and smooth it over and Blake kept saying there was 'no friction' and it was just a 'little incident', but I guess by then the damage had been done.

I knew he had spoken to the press before we came out to the Olympics, saying that the attention on me was hard to deal with and that we were a team. He had a part-time job at the B&Q to make ends meet and had overcome a catalogue of injuries to be there. I guess it was his last chance, he had blown it and he had taken it out on me.

I was really annoyed that headlines were taken by us and not Rebecca Adlington and Joanne Jackson, who had won gold and bronze in the women's freestyle a few hours before our event. There was always a fantastic feeling in the Lodge when anyone won a medal. I hate the fact the press always home in on the negative stuff. I knew I just had to forget about it and focus on the rest of the competition.

The next day I trained as normal and cheered Tonia and Stacie Powell in the Women's 10m synchro event. They dived well, and came in eighth place, with the Chinese taking gold again. Every time the Chinese dived, there was a huge howl from the stadium. Back in the village, Tonia and I went crazy in McDonald's, which was great but it was the only day of eating rubbish for me, as I needed to start thinking about preparing properly for my individual. Mark Foster joined us there, which was a bit bizarre, but he was just lovely and told us he had not had a coach for eight years but had just succeeded on his own, which is incredible.

In the evening, I spent some more time with Mary Beth. I had been told she really liked me and I liked her too. I really wanted to kiss her but in the end I ended up just giving her a peck on the cheek. Back in our apartments, Tonia told me off and said I should have gone for it. Mary Beth texted me telling me to go back, so I ended up walking back to her room alone, and gave her a proper kiss, which was amazing. On my way back to my accommodation I was told off for being in the Americans' accommodation, so I put on an American accent and pretended I was wearing a GB T-shirt. I don't think it worked.

With more than a week before the individual competition, as well as training every day we got to do some fun stuff. One day I watched the gymnastics team compete at the National Indoor Stadium. Ben and Nick Robinson-Baker also competed in the 3m Men's Synchro and they did really well. They should have got fourth but ended up coming seventh, which was very frustrating for them, I think. In the individual springboard event He Chong scored 572. It was a world record and he was so incredible, it was unreal. When he got his medal, he started crying, and Alex Despatie, who got silver, was punching the air. The atmosphere was electric.

After a very offensive 5 a.m. start the next day, we went to the Great Wall of China. We went up in a cable car and took loads of pictures at the top, but the best part was coming back down again in a toboggan. All the supervisors were telling me to slow down. It was brilliant fun! It was also good to learn about the country's history. I cannot believe they carried the rocks two at a time to build it.

In my training sessions, I would do some trampolining, dry-board, abs somersaults and stretch out before going to the pool to practise my list. I felt that 500 was a good benchmark and achievable.

AROUND THIS TIME TEAM GB HAD A REAL RUSH OF GOLD MEDALS IN THE CYCLING, SAILING AND POOL SO THERE WAS A GREAT BUZZ AROUND THE OLYMPIC VILLAGE. IT WAS SUCH A FANTASTIC ATMOSPHERE AND I FELT SO HONOURED TO BE PART OF IT.

Tonia came twelfth in the women's 10m individual prelims, so made it through to the semi-final. She dived really consistently and we all thought she had come fourteenth, but she had actually come in twelfth place again and I picked her up and hugged her really hard. In the final, she was fifth going into the last round but dropped her reverse dive, and ended up in eighth place. I was really happy for her.

I was also able to show Mum and Dad round the village and where I was staying. Dad, like me, thought the best thing was the food hall and the free McDonald's! I showed them all the pictures I had been taking and they bought loads of souvenirs from the special shop. It was really good knowing they were there just outside the village. I spoke to them on the phone, too, with special SIM cards.

One day in the village we chatted to the swimmers, who had competed on the third day and said they were really bored but I could not understand it. In our free time, there always seemed like there was loads to do. I even had my hair cut in the special hairdresser's. Apparently they were trainees and my hair was a bit thin afterwards!

I sorted out my play list for my competition: I chose 'Cold Shoulder' – Basement Jaxx remix; 'I Can Walk on Water I Can Fly' – Basshunter; 'Jumpstyle' – Basshunter; 'Piece Of Me' – Britney Spears (Bimbo Jones remix); 'Trippin on You' – Cahill; 'Forever' – Chris Brown; 'I Just Wanna Make Love to You' – Etta James; 'Sweet About Me' – Gabriella Cilmi; 'What We Gonna Do' – H20; 'No Air' – Jordin Sparks featuring Chris Brown; 'Give It to Me' – Madonna; 'If I Never See Your Face Again' – Maroon 5 featuring Rihanna; 'Disturbia' – Rihanna; 'Who's That Girl' – Robyn; 'Cry for You' – September; 'Take a Bow' – Rihanna Clubland B remix; 'Fix Me' – Velvet; 'Run the Show' – Kat DeLuna; 'Watch Out Alex' – Gaudino featuring Shena; 'All I Ever Wanted' – Basshunter; and 'Groove Coverage' – Poison. This list seems really old now but it was good at the time. After doing that I started to mentally prepare myself as I faced the individual event.

FLYING
THE GB
FLAG

As I started the prelims in the individual event, I was really, really nervous.

AS WE MARCHED ROUND THE POOLSIDE I COULD SEE THE BRITISH GYMNASTICS TEAM, WHO HAD COME TO WATCH, WHICH FELT GREAT, AND SAW MY FAMILY WAVING THEIR FLAG. THROUGHOUT THE EVENT, I GOT REALLY LOUD CHEERS, WHICH HELPED A LOT, AND I COULD DEFINITELY HEAR MY UNCLE KEVIN. I TRIED TO SMILE BEFORE EVERY DIVE, BECAUSE IT WOULD HELP ME RELAX.

In my first dive, I missed my hands slightly, and scored 7 and 7.5s, but made it up with my second dive, the front three and a half somersaults, where I got 8 and 8.5s. My third dive, an inward three and a half, was my best dive. My form in the air was great and I finished high enough to pike out, and execute a good entry with barely a ripple as I landed. I managed to get into my armstand with hardly any wobbles but was still really scared I would come down. My entry was slightly over and I got 7.5s and 8s. My back three and a half started well but was a tiny bit over and my sixth dive, a reverse three and a half somersaults, didn't get a very good start. I jumped a little too far forwards, so was slow and low finishing for 6s. My total score was around 440.40 and twelfth, so just enough to qualify for the semis the following day.

I slept well and was up early. I was desperate to put in a consistent performance. After the parade I sat down and made a point of putting my lucky monkey beside me, and the camera panned over to me where the monkey was sat and I was listening to my iPod with Tonia's pink earphones because I had forgotten mine, which was embarrassing!

I had a shaky start but my fourth-round jump – an armstand back triple somersault with tuck – earned me 86.4 points and put me back in with a chance. I followed that up with a good backward three and a half somersaults, which brought in 89.1 points, and eventually finished eighth on 458.6. I know it wasn't as sharp as it could have been and I was already thinking about the final and improving my performance. Unfortunately Pete, who had a shoulder injury, just missed out by one place, having been in the top ten until his third dive dropped him to thirteenth. There are always surprises and it was a shock that Sascha Klein, who had won the World Cup in February, didn't qualify. After doing some press, Mum and Dad managed to wangle their way onto the bus to see me, which gave me a real lift.

Going into the final later that day, I remember standing on the board and smiling, trying to feel calm and positive. I knew I had to make the most of it. I could see the Union Jacks waving. Chris Hoy, the British cycling and gymnastic teams, and Gordon Brown were all there willing me on. It was going well and, even though I didn't realize it, I was joint fourth after the first round after doing my back two and a half somersaults with one and a half twists piked – one of my most difficult dives – and scoring 81.6.

I continued to do well on both my front three and a half somersaults piked and my inward three and a half somersaults with tuck. However, as the other divers started to do their more difficult dives, I started to drop down the board. After my second dive I was in seventh and then slipped another place after round three, but my fifth dive, a back three and a half somersaults with tuck, gained 84.15 and lifted me back up to sixth.

MY FINAL DIVE, MY REVERSE THREE AND A HALF SOMERSAULTS WITH TUCK, I HAD ONLY LEARNED ABOUT SIX MONTHS EARLIER, SO IT WAS MY NEWEST AND HARDEST DIVE.

I only scored 64.6 and that cost me a place, so I was seventh. Matt Mitcham picked up the gold after his penultimate dive scored 112.10, the highest score of the Games, taking him above China's Zhou Luxin. It was great to see that the Chinese could be beaten and I was delighted with my position.

I was really tired afterwards but had to do loads of press and then pictures and autographs. In the bus on the way back to the village, people were banging on the window giving me things to sign.

When I got back to the GB Lodge, everyone was cheering, which was cool. I stayed with my family for a while and then had to do some interviews live with Gabby Logan. Chris Hoy and a boxer called James DeGale, who won gold in the middleweight category, were also on the sofa and we all had a glass of champagne but I wasn't allowed to drink it.

The following day I was given loads of presents by random Chinese people, including loads of hanging reeds, keyrings and Olympic mascots, which were really cute. As well as Baby Daley I had learnt my Chinese fans had started to call me 'Little Briton' and 'Peking Tom', which are funny nicknames!

I was bursting with excitement about the closing ceremony, because they handed over the Olympic flame to London.

It was similar to the opening ceremony. We had to wait an hour and a half and while we were waiting we drew tattoos on our faces of the British flag and the Olympic rings. As we went to do our lap of honour, the noise was deafening, and the crowd was like a sea of faces. I sat on Ben's shoulders. The show was incredible – a double-decker bus drove in and Leona Lewis came out of it and sang and then David Beckham came out and kicked a ball into the crowd. There was a huge party afterwards. It was such a brilliant feeling to be part of a bigger team. In the GB Lodge they had laid on loads of British nibbles like cheese and pineapple on sticks and sausage rolls. People were dancing and chatting. The divers and the gymnasts stuck together.

We all agreed to meet for an early McDonald's the next day, so at 6 a.m. I found myself ordering a sausage and hash brown, despite the fact I felt really sick. We said goodbye to all the other divers, including the Americans, and headed off to the airport.

Boarding the plane home, Team GB had an entire plane to themselves, so we hadn't yet rejoined the real world. British Airways fitted the plane with a gold nose cone and renamed it 'Pride' after the Team GB mascot. All the gold medallists got upgraded to First Class; I was somewhere in the middle. We spent some time talking to the cabin crew, who asked for our autographs. I felt sad to be going home. It was the best month of my life and I had so many amazing memories. I could not believe I would have to wait for another four years to do it all over again.

When we landed on the tarmac at Heathrow loads of people were waiting for us, including Gordon Brown, Culture Secretary Andy Burnham, Tessa Jowell and loads of press. As we descended the steps all the staff and everyone else were clapping and cheering. Gordon Brown was there and Tessa gave me a massive hug. It was quite surreal.

Walking through the sliding doors into the arrivals area was madness. There were paparazzi and flashing cameras and people everywhere cheering and smiling. We were escorted to a nearby hotel, and as Tonia and I walked in, BBC1 was playing my post-competition interview back.

I WAS SHOCKED TO LEARN HOW MANY PEOPLE HAD WATCHED MY EVENT – 1.3 BILLION!

It's not really a number you can comprehend. It was overwhelming. Some of the other athletes met their families and it was lovely to see some emotional reunions as people met their loved ones. Mum and Dad had flown home with the rest of the family a few days earlier, so had gone straight home to Plymouth. I didn't mind, though, as I was so busy and knew I would see them soon. Everyone wanted autographs and pictures and I had to do another round of TV chats.

After a few hours, I was exhausted and relieved when Tonia, Andy and I left the group to make the drive back to Plymouth. As we sped along the motorway, we were quiet and thoughtful. I promised myself I would come back stronger, more focused and more consistent in four years' time with a harder list of dives. I would throw every last bit of energy and determination I had into it.

COMING
HOME

'WE WENT CAMEL RIDING AND SAND DUNING
AS WELL, WHICH WERE AMAZING EXPERIENCES.
WE ALSO TOOK SOME INCREDIBLE PICTURES OF
US ALL DOING SYNCHRONIZED SOMERSAULTS
TOGETHER IN THE SURF.'

Back in Plymouth, everyone wanted to congratulate me and hear about my time in Beijing. The invites started to come in thick and fast and I attended the EA launch party for the Tiger Woods PGA Tour 2009 game, where I met Rupert Grint and other stars of *Harry Potter*, plus Ashley Cole and Dizzee Rascal. I was also interviewed on the TV show, *Sound*, and met McFly and the presenters Annie Mac and Nick Grimshaw.

IT FELT QUITE STRANGE THAT EVERYONE WANTED ME AT THEIR DIFFERENT EVENTS, BUT I LOVED GOING TO LONDON AND MEETING ALL THE PEOPLE I HAD ONLY SEEN ON TV.

OPPOSITE

Me and my new

celeb pals!

A few weeks after that, I attended a completely different event: the Pride of Britain Awards. On the red carpet everyone was screaming my name and I actually felt what it must be like to be a celebrity – very weird. It was a really heart-warming event and a special experience to hear about the inspirational people who won awards. I also met stars like Geri Halliwell, Richard Branson, Joan Collins and Dannii Minogue. I made sure I got as many photos as possible to add to my collection, which is one of the reasons that I would never refuse anyone a picture now, as I know what it is like to be on the other side.

The attention from girls also seemed to ramp up a gear. I don't think I could ever get tired of the female attention but it's a bit overwhelming when you just want to be with your friends, and sometimes the girls are quite freaky. They come and scream in my face and I never know what to say. Some of them are quite attractive but it's the prettier ones that don't come up because they are normally the cooler ones. Soon after, someone posted a link on my Facebook wall to a YouTube video of a girl singing 'I Kissed a Girl' by Katy Perry, but instead of 'girl', it was 'Tom Daley' and she rewrote all the words with lines like 'Tom is hot like

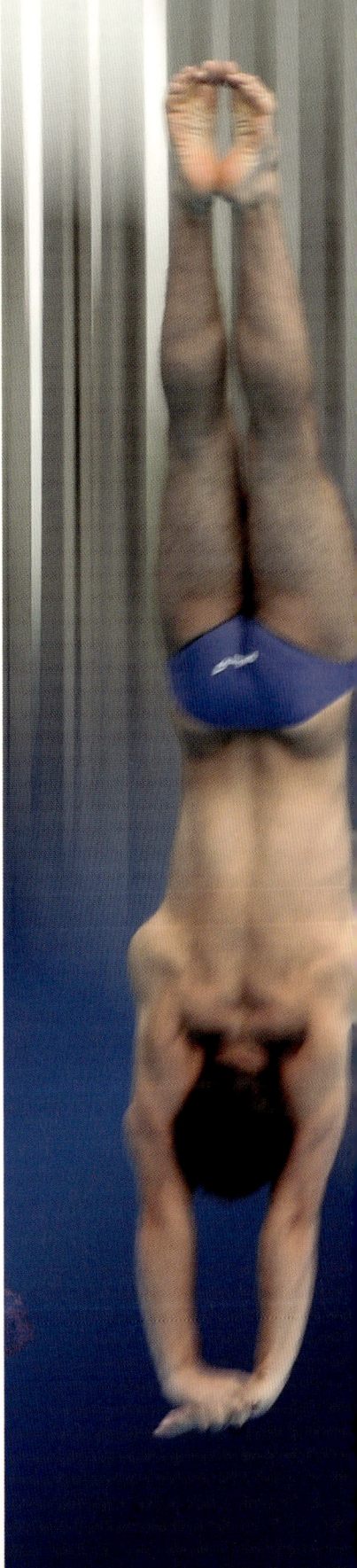

hell, it's not his fault', 'He was just a seven placer but for me he is a winner' and 'Tom's got a hot body and we cannot blame him for that'. I thought it was a joke at first – but it wasn't! Underneath she'd written 'Sorry for my voice'. It was hilarious – if a little bit freaky.

OPPOSITE
My diving partner, Max Brick, heading for the water.

Heading back to school in September just felt really normal and it was good to see my friends and catch up with everyone after the holidays. Some of the new Year 7 girls kept asking me for my autograph, which was a bit weird. Tonia actually created my autograph for me, when I was just ten. We were messing around at training one day and she told me I could not have a boring signature that anyone was able to copy and that I needed a decent one, so she wrote it and I copied it. It has been my signature ever since.

I started my GCSEs: Maths, two English, two Science, four IT and Spanish, and later, when I moved to Plymouth College, I added Photography to that list.

I was back to competing very quickly and at the end of September I headed to Germany for the FINA World Junior Championships, where I won two silver medals in the fourteen- to fifteen-year-old age group. It was the first time I had competed in the event because before I was too young. I scored five perfect 10s for my back three and a half somersaults with tuck and got a personal best of 549.60, which was great but not quite good enough, unfortunately. It was the first time I had competed against Chinese diver Qiu Bo and he just beat me with 551.85 points.

I HAD NEVER SEEN QIU AT A COMPETITION BEFORE BUT HE HAD A HARDER LIST THAN I DID AND WAS CONSISTENTLY LANDING ON HIS HEAD. I COULD NOT BELIEVE THERE WAS YET ANOTHER CHINESE DIVER IN THE MIX. I FELT MY MENTALITY START TO CHANGE; I WASN'T JUST DOING IT FOR THE EXPERIENCE, I WAS GOING FOR GOLD.

I also had a go at the springboard and picked up another silver medal with 485.25 points.

16 October 2009 is a date that will stick in my head for a long time. I had the day off school to take part in the parade around London with 500 members of Olympic and Paralympic Team GB, including the sixty-nine medallists. It was a really bright and sunny day and we could not believe how many people had come to watch us. Trafalgar Square was completely packed out with people waving Union Jacks and foam hands; it was like a huge sea of heads and it was so noisy! All the medallists were on the first bus and I was on the second bus with Tonia, Blake and the rest of the diving team. I was pleased that Blake and I could put everything that had happened behind us. We were still diving together and were planning to compete together again the following February.

Everyone was waving and cheering and taking pictures of us; it was like we were gods. The atmosphere was amazing and I kept thinking, 'If this is the spirit of the people and the Olympic Games isn't even in London, I cannot imagine what it's going to be like in 2012.'

Even on holiday my favourite place is in the pool! I always spend hours with my brothers, larking about.

In the evening we went to Buckingham Palace, where we met the Queen. Buckingham Palace is massive and everyone there was so posh. They were bringing loads of food round on silver trays, including caviar. We all looked very smart, too, in our Olympic suits. We were standing in the room where they give out knighthoods, mixing with all the other Olympic athletes, and officials were circulating telling us how to behave towards the Queen to acknowledge that she was there, that we needed to say 'Good evening, your Majesty' or 'Your Royal Highness'. The men were told to nod their heads and the girls to do a small curtsey. We were told not to give her our hands to shake, unless she went to shake our hand first.

She met all the medallists first and apparently said she wanted to meet the divers next. I was at the front of the queue. She came over and proffered a hand in a white glove for me to shake. She was really small and spoke so quietly, I could barely hear her. She has such lovely features and it was real honour to meet her.

I nodded my head, greeting her with 'Your Royal Highness'. She said well done and keep working hard for 2012, before moving down the line.

Blake was at the end. As she went to speak to him, he did a huge curtsey and nodded his head so much he almost head-butted her. Only Blake could do that! It was so funny. Tonia caught my eye and I was puffing my cheeks out, trying so hard not to laugh.

Afterwards I was allowed a bit of a break and was able to spend some time with my family. We went to Florida for a week's holiday. It was great to get away from it all and just be a typical family and we stayed in a great hotel. We went to Universal Studios and I took part in the Blue Horizons show at Seaworld. I did some dives off the board before the show started to get some British people to watch and later signed autographs. I also swam with dolphins and met a killer whale called Shamru. They made the whales splash me with water for some pictures and I smelt of fish for the rest of the day! We got to go to the other parks and spent our time going on rollercoaster rides and having a complete ball.

It was then back to school and training as normal. I had a good few months to get some schoolwork under my belt and trained religiously at the pool, day in day out. Some of my friends had started having parties and drinking but I didn't feel like I was missing out. I would go to parties if I was at home and drink Coke or just go to the cinema or to the beach with my friends on my day off. I didn't mind the sacrifices I was making.

I could tell Christmas was approaching when I switched on the Christmas lights in Plymouth. Tonia and girl group Bad Lashes (from *The X Factor*) were also switching them on. There was lots of screaming. We never got to actually touch the switch – Bad Lashes did it together while Tonia and I hovered at the back of the stage. Afterwards there was some slightly awkward dancing with the Lord Mayor.

At the beginning of December I won the *Herald* Sports Award for Young Sports Personality of the Year and the South-West Sports Star of the Year. We always have two big tables now and it's a regular event in the Daley calendar.

Another highlight of my month was introducing George Sampson at the Royal Variety Performance. It was a great honour to be asked to do that and a great experience for me. I met so many different people: Leona Lewis, Duffy, Take That, Jimmy Carr and Michael McIntyre. The one person who I thought was a bit of a diva was Rihanna. I asked her for a photo and she ignored me. When I meet any celebrities I always think they are much smaller than I imagine them to be – apart from Rihanna, that is, who is really tall! I feel so much more nervous about the presenting than I do about my diving.

I was thinking in my head, 'There are Royals in the box, you can't mess

this up. Just read the autocue, you CAN read, so just read!' It went really smoothly after that.

I was also honoured to be nominated for Young Sports Personality of the Year again, the award I won the previous year. It was won by paralympic gold medallist Ellie Simmonds, who thoroughly deserved it. Ellie was also at Beijing and the youngest member of the Paralympic GB team, and she matched Rebecca Adlington's double gold medals in the pool. It was the first time I'd been to the event and it was incredible because there were so many sports stars there and everyone talks to each other about their disciplines. I was starting to have to wear more suits and smart clothes. My first suit was from Next but later Burberry started dressing me.

I really enjoyed Christmas and had a lovely time with my family. I had four days off but then was back to full training. My 2009 began with a party at our house with my cousins, Sam and Joe. We had a Chinese takeaway and saw the New Year in together. I always joke that in order to beat the Chinese I need to eat like them! It wasn't a big party or anything but it was just nice to spend some time with us all together.

2009 kicked off with a very interesting photoshoot at the National Marine Aquarium in Plymouth for the *Daily Mail* photographer Andy Hooper. I had a good relationship with Andy and had given him a set of pictures that I had taken during the Olympics of Tonia and me messing around in the Olympic Village, and which he had published with funny captions in the newspaper. Mum had been told it was just in a tank with a few fish but when I arrived it turned out that I was going to be shot in the biggest shark tank in Europe. There were more than 1,000 fish and three twelve-foot sand sharks circling around. They looked absolutely huge. Apparently their names were Emily, Enzo and Howardine, which sounded friendly enough. Dad looked particularly nervous.

'Do they bite?' I asked

'Not normally, no. But they can,' one of the shark handlers replied. There were two scuba divers and a free diver there, just in case. Eek!

It was about eight degrees and I was in my trunks. Andy was by the glass in the spectator area and I was told to dive down and put my

'THERE WERE MORE THAN 1,000 FISH AND THREE TWELVE-FOOT SAND SHARKS CIRCLING AROUND. THEY LOOKED ABSOLUTELY HUGE.'

hands up against the glass while the sharks were in the distance. I gingerly climbed in. It was freezing. I dived down to where he had told me to and could see Andy snapping away. A few seconds in and I saw all the people behind him take a collective gasp and start pointing and shrieking. I could hear the muffled shouts. I whipped my head round and this huge shark was coming towards me. It was like everything was going in slow motion. My heart was in my mouth. I shot to the surface as quickly as I could and tucked my legs up as far as I could underneath me and this huge shark swam so fast under me, almost brushing my legs. As I panted at the surface, Andy asked me to go down . . . again!

The trainers were there fending the sharks off with sticks. I have never been so scared in my life. They made me go down another eight times. I was so relieved when that shoot was over. The photos looked pretty good, although at first my friends thought it could not be real, but it definitely was.

February began with the British Diving Championships in Sheffield. It was actually snowing when we arrived and I could not believe how much snow there was everywhere – it was two feet deep. I built a funny snowman with Tonia and Brooke. I was delighted after picking up the gold medal with 517 points. Jack Laugher from Harrogate Diving Club finished in second place. I only had a few weeks before I was competing again as I took part in the Armada Cup in Plymouth. I won all three boards in my own age group and it was fantastic to compete in my hometown. Jack was second in all of my events again. Comedian Justin Lee Collins came to watch the event and I was able to meet him afterwards. He was there for one of his programmes, *Justin Lee Collins: High Diver*, in which he was learning to dive for one of the FINA Series competitions. Leon was coaching him but he ended up perforating one of his eardrums so wasn't able to dive, but he took part in a mini competition instead.

Three weeks later I was working for my sponsor Adidas modelling their new running kit for a photo shoot in their London store. I was getting used to being in front of the cameras. The photographers always tell you to look down and keep your chin up but I never really had to do any crazy poses or anything.

The next day I attended a party for a young girl who was recently diagnosed with cancer. She was going into hospital for treatment but had a special party before then to spend time with family and friends. The whole issue of cancer is so close to my heart, I cannot do enough and was more than happy to give up my time to be there.

A few days later I was on my way to Qatar for a World Series competition. It was fine but unfortunately I didn't make the final. If I had been in the other semi-final group, I would have, which is frustrating – it just depends what group you end up in. While the team were out there, we went shopping to this amazing mall that was meant to look like Venice with waterways running through it and the ceiling was painted to look like the sky, which was pretty crazy. We went camel riding and sand duning as well, which were amazing experiences. We also took some incredible pictures of us all doing synchronized

somersaults together in the surf. Tonia could not come with us because she had hurt her knee, so we put a photo of her face on a wooden spoon and took her everywhere with us and took silly pictures and sent them back to her. We stuck the spoon on top of a camel, out of the neck of a GB T-shirt and in a random traffic cone. We left her in the desert so she's probably burnt to a crisp now!

Changzhou in China was our next stop for the second leg of the FINA World Series competition at the end of March. I won my semi-final with a fab score of 532.95, beating the reigning Olympic champion, Matthew Mitcham, into third place and went one better in the final, where I eventually finished third with a new personal best of 540.70 behind Qiu Bo on 542.25 and Zhou Luxin on 560. I was really pleased with my performance as it was improving.

The Chinese competitions are very regimented and outside the events there is never that much to do because we are normally in the non-touristy parts. The training facilities are always amazing so we make the most of them, and when we're not training we try and amuse ourselves as best we can, although Facebook and a lot of other websites are banned by the government there. I know a few words in Chinese now, like 'Hello' and 'Good luck', so I can talk to my fellow competitors.

After a break with my family at our caravan in Watergate Bay, it was straight up to Sheffield for the third FINA World Series event. I was really looking forward to competing on home soil and it was also the first event I'd compete in with Max Brick. Blake and I had ended our diving partnership after Blake got punched outside a nightclub three days before we were expected to compete in synchro at the British Championships in February. He had two black eyes and a broken nose, needed ten stitches, and claimed it was an unprovoked attack and everyone hated him after the incident in Beijing. After coming home, he said that he had had death threats on Facebook and abusive emails blaming him for our result. Somehow, I felt that it made me look like the bad guy again. Every time he was mentioned in the press it was always as Tom Daley's partner and it was often negative, and Dad rang Andy and said in no uncertain terms that he didn't want me diving with him again as he was a bad influence. A few names were bandied about, including James Milton and Max, and it was decided that Max and I had the best chance. I had known him for years on the diving circuit and, because we were similar ages, we got on really well. It was more like diving with a friend and training was always fun.

Max and I finished in sixth place in the synchro and in my individual competition I clocked up another new personal best score after getting 10s in four of my six dives to score 540.885. Unfortunately I was nudged into second place by China's Huo Liang by a mere 0.60 and I edged Qiu into third place by 0.35 points and Matt came fourth. I was learning that the Chinese hate it when you put pressure on them – for them, being right on their tail is the thing that makes them panic and mess up. It was a really high standard so I was chuffed. But it was becoming clearer and clearer that while I could execute my list almost to perfection, I would have to start learning new, harder dives to remain competitive because my degree of difficulty was still lower than those of the other top divers.

Later that month I went on a plane to Florida for a ten-day-long training camp at Coral Springs. The training went really well out there but about halfway through our trip we had to stay in the hotel because swine flu had broken out. We ended up spending a lot of time in the pool, taking pictures of human towers, doing Superman impressions off the boards and generally trying to amuse ourselves.

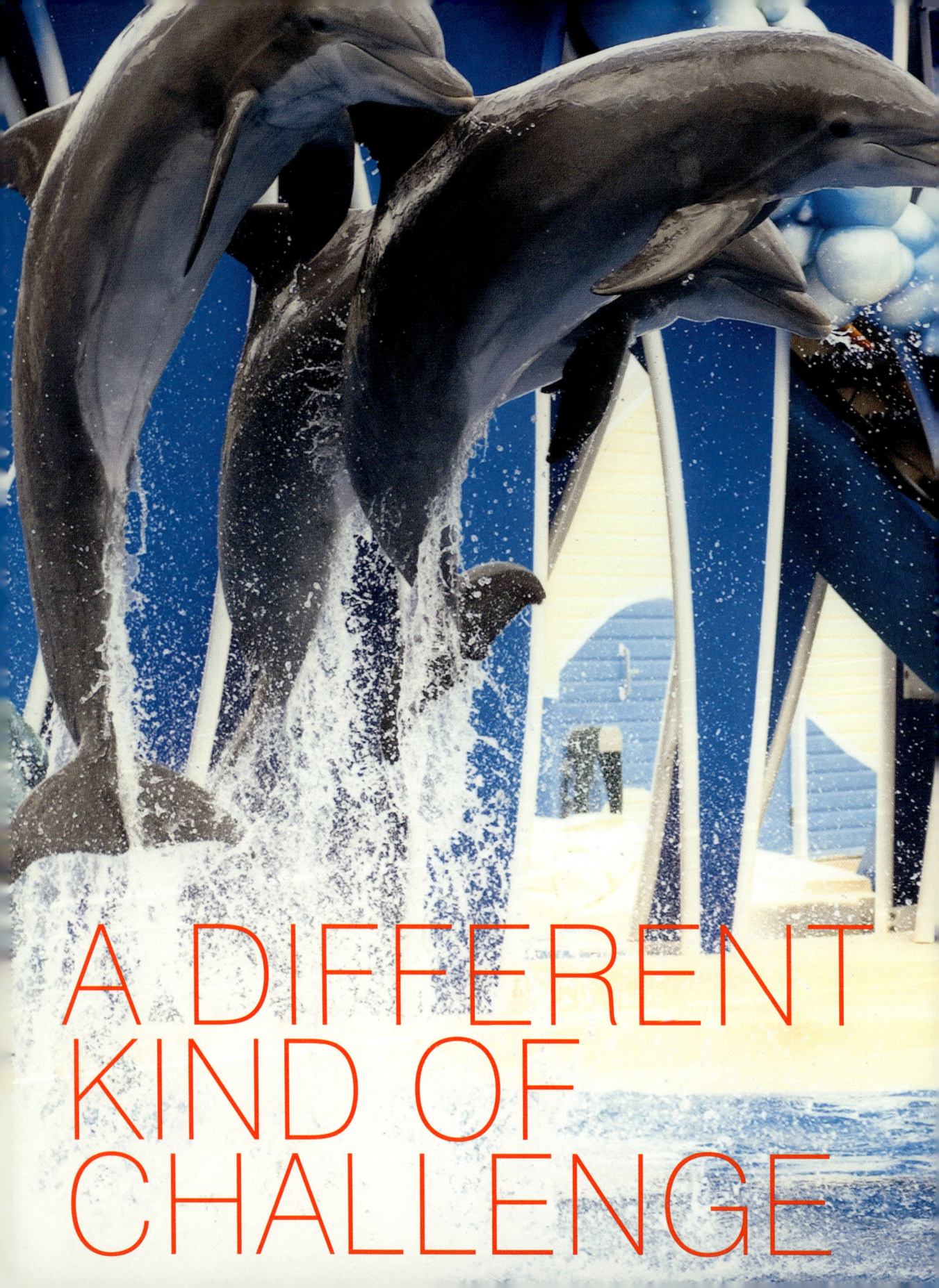

A DIFFERENT KIND OF CHALLENGE

When I went to school at Eggbuckland Community College, I was quite mischievous, maybe a little bit naughty. I was silly during lessons and a bit of a class clown. I was on report quite a lot for singing in lessons and stuff like that. One day during science class I was walking stupidly, flicking my feet. It was un-cool to do up your shoelaces so they were undone and I was walking up and down flicking my feet like a soldier, thinking I was cool. My shoe flicked off my foot, flew across the classroom and landed in the science experiment that my teacher was doing at the front, splashing her. I can't remember what was in the experiment – it wasn't anything too bad – but I could have died from embarrassment.

One of the girls in my group of friends, Harriet Jones, was the one who was so naughty but she never got caught or she blamed it on someone else. In our little gang Nikita was the one who always got upset when we got caught, Sophie screamed a lot and Alex was the lookout guy. Quite often at lunchtimes, we used to have food fights with fruit across the courtyard. We would bring in loads of apples and melons and hide them in our bags until break-time. It was a total fruit fest! Eventually, they used to ban selling fruit from the canteen and everyone got told off. But we didn't stop – we used to take our fruit into our classroom, which was two floors up, and wait for the year above to walk below us, then throw oranges and squirty yoghurts at them.

The bullying crept up really slowly. Lots of people called me 'Diver Boy' and that didn't worry me. When some of the older boys started calling me 'Speedo Boy' after the Olympics, I thought it was an amusing nickname. I thought it would gradually tail off but it slowly got worse and worse. Mum and Dad told me that some name-calling and stuff was to be expected and to try and let it go over my head, which I did.

In the months after coming home from Beijing, if the weather was good we would sometimes go and sit out in the field, but I started to get rugby tackled every time I went out. The first few times it happened, I was annoyed but laughed it off. In my head, I thought that messing around like that was what boys did to each other. But after a while I started to feel nervous and paranoid. It was like I never had any space to go anywhere or do anything and be left alone.

I HAD TOLD MY PARENTS ABOUT MY WORRIES FROM THE START AND, LIKE ME, THEY WERE MORE CONCERNED ABOUT THE PHYSICAL SIDE.

In the classroom the bullies did stupid stuff, like throwing masking tape at my head. Not long into the new term I had a media day with five interviews and I let slip that I was sometimes called Speedo Boy and that someone had jokingly said, 'How much are your legs worth? I'll break them for you', before he rugby tackled me. I told the journalist that it was just banter and I thought it was normal. But then of course he published the words 'Tom Daley is being bullied', which was picked up everywhere, and with ammunition and the knowledge that it was getting to me it got much, much worse.

One of my biggest annoyances was that people didn't accept my sport. To my group of friends I was just Tom, with or without my diving. They understood how hard I needed to train and what diving means to me, but I felt other people thought it was a game, or some stupid hobby, which they could not take seriously. I just wanted to blend in with everyone else and get on with my schoolwork. I've always been focused academically and, as with diving, tried to do my best. Looking back, I can see that they were probably jealous, but it didn't feel like it then. It was hell. I would bottle it up until I got home and then collapse in floods of tears. When I went training, if I was having a bad session it would make everything worse and I would feel awful. Some days, if everything was going brilliantly in my diving it would make me forget about it.

Mum went down to the school a few times and tried to speak to the teachers, who said they were sorting it out. But it was hard for them because it wasn't any individual or group in particular. Sometimes it seemed like it was almost everyone. The younger kids started copying the older ones. In the end they gave my friends and me a classroom that we could retreat to at break-times and we would sit and chat while having our lunch. But I suppose maybe the bullies thought I was getting special treatment.

IT WAS MOSTLY INSTIGATED BY PEOPLE IN THE YEARS ABOVE, MAINLY THE HARDER GUYS, AND IT WAS QUITE INTIMIDATING AT TIMES. A TYPICAL DAY WOULD START WITH ME WAKING UP AND THE FIRST THING I WOULD THINK WAS THAT I DIDN'T WANT TO GO TO SCHOOL, THAT I DIDN'T WANT ANOTHER ROUND OF ABUSE AND NAME-CALLING. I FELT EVERYONE HATED ME.

As I walked through the school gates, my heart would be banging against my ribcage and my hands would be clammy. I felt like everyone was always looking and pointing at me and being mean. As I was walking down the corridor to lessons someone would try and trip me up, and when I finally got to my desk, someone would snatch my pencil case and empty it.

My friends would help me pick my stuff up and tell whoever did it to pick it up but they would shoot back, 'I'm not picking it up, it's his pencil case.'

One day someone threw a roll of Sellotape at my head really hard and I had a massive lump. It really stung but I had to pretend it was nothing.

My friends would help me. They thought we were getting through it together. They stuck with me during break-times and lunchtimes and we would just sit and try to be as normal as possible. I started to learn that as soon as I went outside people would start being idiots. If I went onto the field, I would have to make sure I sat down in the middle of the group, so I could not be rugby tackled. Or we would try and find a quiet corner, where I would cower and hope that no one noticed me.

But I didn't always have my close friends with me and I became more and more worried about being physically hurt. When the boys kept saying, 'I'll break your legs,' I got more worried that they were deliberately trying to hurt me. If I was badly injured it would have a major knock-on effect on my diving. I just could not let that happen, but I felt so powerless.

One day, we were on the field at lunchtime because it was so sunny, and as soon as the bell went I stood up and immediately was tackled by a fairly big guy and landed awkwardly on my wrist. It swelled up and it was really sore to touch. I wasn't allowed to land hands first during my diving for five days and I started to worry about competitions.

'I can't do it. I don't want to be there, I can't go back,' I told Mum and Dad. And it was then that they made the decision to pull me out of school. They were furious and felt that despite the promises, the problems were not being dealt with by the school.

I had a couple of days left before the Easter holidays and then went on a training camp and then on to the FINA Grand Prix in Florida. Knowing that I wasn't going back, I instantly felt calm and more relaxed and it was evident in my diving. It was an outdoor competition and I enjoy being outside. Other divers find diving in the open air harder – because as well as spotting the water, you need to spot the sky and it can become confusing. It's always quite hard to tell the difference between the water and the sky. Normally they will have jet sprays going across the water, which helps you spot the difference because the water is constantly moving. The Chinese divers in particular do not do as well outside because they do so many repetitions indoors that when they get outside it feels too different.

My grandparents, Jenny and Doug, had been on holiday in Florida and they came to watch and brought some friends. In recent years we have started calling Grandma Jenny 'Jenny Wrinkles'. Meeting them on the poolside, one of the friends asked if I thought I could win.

'No way,' I replied, convinced I didn't stand a chance against the tough competition.

However, it was my day and I beat Sascha Klein and Zhou Luxin to the gold medal. My score was 554.90 and my backward three and a half somersaults got 10s across the board. It was the fifth time that year I had beaten my previous personal best. I felt fantastic and, better than that, I still felt that there was more to come.

During half-term and on the day of my fifteenth birthday, we were invited back to Seaworld, where I opened a new ride, the Manta ride, a rollercoaster where after being strapped into the seat and tilted forwards, so you are going head first, it climbed to the dizzy heights of 140ft before soaring down again, where we were sprayed by water – it really felt like I was flying, it was incredible. The sensation of falling through the air was actually a bit like diving. In the evening we had a special meal at the Rainforest Café.

I know my parents considered a number of options for my schooling, including home schooling. Because of the press and the fact people knew about the problems I was having at Eggbuckland, there were various offers from other schools. When I arrived home from Florida my parents told me that we were going on a tour around Plymouth College because I had been offered a scholarship there. I loved it. The ancient buildings were like something out of Harry Potter's Hogwarts and they had loads of athletes there. They told me that the school was geared towards elite sport. They had loads of swimmers there, including Cassie Pattern, who had won a bronze at Beijing. They told me that they could gear my academic programme around my diving and be completely flexible, which was a dream.

Having to make the decision to leave Eggbuckland was one of the toughest decisions I have ever had to make. I met up with my schoolfriends and got really upset because I was worried I would never see them again. They told me to grab the opportunity with both hands.

As soon as I went to Plymouth College I decided it should be a new start. The environment was totally different. Everyone there obviously really wanted to learn and be there, rather than mess around and have fun. I was so grateful for the scholarship, and was determined to do my best.

I was horribly nervous on my first day but I needn't have been because I slotted in immediately and made new friends quickly. I found it much easier to make male friends there. At Eggbuckland, I found it far more difficult to make male friends because they didn't seem as fun and easy-going as the girls. But at Plymouth College there are a group of guys I now hang around with, like the swimmers Joe Patching, Aaron Rickhuss and Jordan Sharples. They really understood how hard it is to balance training with schoolwork. I finally felt that I could be anonymous, and had it not been for the school I know I would not have done so well academically, or in my diving. I will always be grateful for that opportunity.

As soon as I started I had ten days to learn the whole syllabus for a science GCSE exam, but the teachers were brilliant and gave me one-to-one tuition and got me up to speed very quickly. At the end of June, my new school held an activity week and I had a great time trying some new sports like surfing, kayaking, sailing and mountain biking. At the end of that year I signed a contract to say I would not do any extreme sports, in case of injury.

I finished school for the year on 3 July and the next day I had synchronized diving training with my new diving partner, Max. The first day was in Plymouth and the next was in Southampton. Training was going well, and with just a few weeks until the World Championships we needed to put the hours in. This was when I decided to do no media so I could focus solely on my diving. I was training twice a day for about five hours. I also went to watch my brother Ben in his school play, *The Wizard of Oz*. He was in the choir. I always try to support my brothers as much as they support me.

BEING
CROWNED
WORLD
CHAMP

'BEING WITH THE TEAM
IS ALWAYS FUN AND
DURING THAT TRIP
THE SYNCHRONIZED
SWIMMERS TAUGHT
US A ROUTINE IN OUR
DOWNTIME.'

My Rome adventure started on the 10 July when I flew to Italy for a ten-day training camp before the competition. The weather was glorious – there wasn't a cloud in the sky. I have always dived better outside – Andy jokes that I am solar-powered! I always feel better and dive better when I have a tan.

Being with the team is always fun and during that trip the synchronized swimmers taught us a routine in our downtime.

DIVING IS QUITE A BIG SPORT IN ITALY AND THE STANDS AT THE FORO ITALICO WHERE WE WERE COMPETING WERE PACKED OUT. THEY WERE CHEERING ME TOO, WHICH FELT REALLY GOOD. I ENDED UP COMING FIFTH IN THE PRELIMS, WHICH WAS QUITE GOOD CONSIDERING I THOUGHT I WASN'T DIVING VERY WELL.

The semi-final kicked off at 10 a.m. the next morning. I hate mornings but I knew I needed to get into the top twelve. I started to step up a level and came away in third place. I knew I would need to execute my whole list almost perfectly to get a medal because my tariff was still lower than all the other divers. My hope was that I would dive well and put pressure on them, and they would then make mistakes. After Fort Lauderdale I felt really confident – but I still didn't think I would get anywhere near the top of the leaderboard.

I scored 8s for my first dive; it wasn't bad but I knew I needed to get a cleaner entry. My second dive was the front three and a half. I can remember taking off and thinking, 'I need to go for it'. I got my entry and was rewarded with 9s and 9.5s, so I was very happy with that. The next one was my inward three and a half tuck, which is one of my weaker dives, but I scored 9s on it. It was good but I jumped quite far away from the board, which lost me marks. I saw the rankings on the board halfway.

I was in fourth place but one point off the medals and knew I could pull myself back up.

I HAD MY ARMSTAND BACK TRIPLE TUCK NEXT, AND WHEN I WAS IN MY HANDSTAND I TALKED MYSELF THROUGH IT, COUNTING 'ONE, TWO, THREE', THEN WENT. I WAS DETERMINED TO BE REALLY PRECISE SO THE JUDGES COULD SEE HOW HARD I WAS TRYING. AS I LANDED, I VACUUMED THE WATER DOWN WITH ME AND WAS AWARDED WITH A 10 AND 9.5S, BUT I WAS STILL 11 POINTS AWAY FROM THE MEDALS.

Then I had the back three and a half tuck, which is the dive I scored flat 10s on in America. I knew I needed to do an exact replica – and I did! I scored four tens, which gave me maximum marks. Suddenly I had overtaken Zhou Luxin and was in third place. I was seven points off Matt, who was in second and 12 points of Qiu, who was in the top spot.

I walked to the edge of the board. Zhou had gone before me and scored 9s. The board told me I needed a 9.2 average to be first. He was in fourth and I knew I needed to do something more than that to get ahead of the others. They were all doing the two and a half somersaults, two and a half twists – which had a higher tariff, 3.6, to my reverse three and a half somersaults, which was 3.4.

I was nervous but as my toes touched the end of the board, I thought, 'Shit or bust, here I go.' I counted to three, took a deep breath and threw every ounce of energy I had left into the dive. I was spinning round, willing myself to see every single point and then kicking out, everything pointed, straight and stretched.

As I hit the water I knew immediately that it was a great dive which would give me a medal. I was sucked under the surface of the pool.

I felt so happy it was as if I could fly. I could hear the muffled cheers and wolf whistles and I wanted to get to the surface as quickly as possible. I was so elated. I felt like I could walk on water.

Waiting for the scores to come up was painful – even though it was probably only three seconds. And then they were there.

9.5. 9.5 10 10 9.5 10 10

It was enough to give me a medal – and brought my total to 539.85.

'Yes! I've got a World Championship medal,' I yelled, hugging Andy. Everyone was congratulating me on poolside and Tonia and the rest of the team were jumping up and down. It was such an unbelievable feeling.

Gemma Field, the media coordinator, led me towards the mixed zone to talk to the cameras.

'Amazing. Well done, Tom, you've got a bronze,' she said. As we started walking away I had my back to the pool and there was a collective gasp from the crowd. I spun round and saw that Matt had missed his dive and had gone over. Then the scores came up – there was a massive cheer – I was still in the lead. Amazing – a silver medal!

'Let me watch this dive just in case,' I said to Gemma.

'OK, just in case,' she laughed.

'Well, it's not going to happen again, is it,' I smiled. Qiu only needed 8s to win the gold medal at that point – scores that he had exceeded in every dive up until then.

He took off, and as he spun round, he edged sideways and then landed with an almighty splash.

'Oh my god, what is happening?' I said. I could barely breathe – it was like I had been winded. It felt like an eternity as we waited for the scores to come up. I had my head in my hands. He got 7s and 7.5s.

THE ITALIANS WENT CRAZY. EVERYONE WAS CHEERING. IT WAS SUCH A SURREAL EXPERIENCE – IT WAS ALMOST LIKE IT WAS HAPPENING TO SOMEONE ELSE. I WAS STUNNED.

I felt completely dazed and suddenly I was face to face with an Italian lady doing a live TV interview. She started questioning me in Italian – I didn't know what to say. The team came over and were giving me hugs. I just wanted to see my dad but it was chaotic. We went to get the medals and everyone was singing the National Anthem and the British flag went up above my head. I always thought I would cry if I became World Champion but I didn't. My cheeks ached from smiling so much.

After that I went straight to the mixed zone and then to the press conference. After answering a few questions, I saw my dad coming in at the back and all of a sudden, I saw his hand go up.

'What IS he doing?' I thought, slightly alarmed.

'I'd like to ask a question,' he said.

'Can you please tell me which publication you are from?' the Italian compere asked.

'I'm Tom's dad. Tom, can you give me a cuddle?'

Typical Dad! I was so embarrassed but didn't want to look like a heartless idiot, so shuffled over.

'Come on, please, come on,' he said, seeing my blushes.

I gave him a massive cuddle and he wrapped his flag around me. He was sobbing.

The surrounding journalists had burst into a spontaneous round of applause.

'Dad's amazing – he takes me to training every day. But this is embarrassing!' I added.

'No, it's not!'

'Yes it is, Dad, oh God … I'll see you later,' I told him, before walking back to the front. My cheeks were burning.

After that there were reports about him being pushy. Anyone who knew Dad knows what he was like. He used to say, 'I taught him how to ride a bike; I changed his nappies. What father would not go in and see his son when he'd just been crowned World Champion?'

Everyone made out that it was as if he'd tied up the security guard, scaled the fence and tunnelled in – but actually he'd just come to find me, and stumbled across the room. He could not understand that everyone else got to say well done to me before he did. It was his emotions coming out; he was just happy for me. I then knew to ring him first before I did anything else. Mum was equally happy watching at home; apparently the neighbours saw her jumping up and down on

the sofa! She said it was like fifty Christmases as a child rolled into one.

All the team were so good to me after my win, the first thing Max said to me was: 'I'm going to be standing next to a World Champion.' My phone didn't stop ringing and I had to do lots of interviews. I didn't care because I felt I could speak about the experience forever.

A completely surreal moment – I didn't expect to, but winning was mind-blowing.

The following morning, as I opened my eyes, I was convinced I had been dreaming. I didn't want to let myself think I had actually won because I really wasn't sure whether it was real. Stepping out of my room, I immediately saw Tonia and Brooke.

'Hey World Champion,' they chorused. And then I felt amazing.

Three days after that we had our synchro event. I found it quite difficult coming off the high from earlier in the week and focusing on competing again – normally the synchro is before the individual.

We made it through to the final, but were inconsistent, and after a particularly bad third dive, which dropped us down to last, we ended up in ninth place. We were not disappointed, we just knew we needed to be more consistent. It still felt like a relatively new partnership and we had scored high points for one of the dives, which hopefully showed we had potential together.

Going home is always good. I was looking forward to flopping on the sofa and catching up with my friends. Walking into the house, I saw the kitchen door was shut, which was strange as it was always open.

'Why is the door shut, Mum?'

'William's probably in there eating something he shouldn't,' she said.

As I opened the door, everyone shouted, 'Surprise!' I was really shocked. All my friends from school, Andy, Tonia and Brooke, and all the family had come. We toasted my success. I still could not quite believe I was World Champion at fifteen. My Aunty Marie had baked me a cake in the shape of a gold medal, which was cool. Plymouth was also celebrating and a couple of days later a civic reception with the Lord Mayor was held and I was taken around the town on an open-top bus and along the Royal Parade with everyone cheering. Nikita and Sophie were getting the bus into town in front of me, waving and pulling stupid faces. Highlights of the event were shown on the enormous screen and I did a short interview. It felt really good that I had put my city on the map. I was also given a gold *Blue Peter* badge for exceptional achievements. David Beckham, J. K. Rowling and the Queen have them too, apparently.

August was a slightly calmer month for me and we are always given a few weeks off from training after the competition season has finished. I opened a new Adidas store before doing the family holiday to Alicante in Spain. We were there for two weeks and it was great to spend some time with my mum, dad and brothers. The weather was fantastic so I was able to play in the sea and pool with my brothers. This time was needed after all the excitement of the World Diving Championships.

After my success in Italy, I was told that an Italian magazine wanted to shoot me for a feature on British stars.

'I'm going to do a photoshoot,' I told Tonia and Brooke, during one of our daily training sessions.
'Who for?'
'Vogu,' I said, 'or something stupid like that.'
'What?'
'Yeah, Vog.'
'Do you mean *Vogue*?'
'Yeah.'
'Oh my god.'
'And it's with Kate Moss!'
'What?!'

The theme of the shoot was learning to swim. We shot it at the run-down Queen Mother's Sports Centre near Victoria station in London, and Bruce Weber was shooting it. It was the first time I'd been shot by such a big-name photographer. I was doing a photography GCSE so I had studied his work and could not wait to see a snapper like him in action. I got there first and Kate came out to the pool and said, 'Hi, Tom!' She's got a real South London voice.

'Well done in the Olympics. It was great. We were watching you.'
'Thanks.' I was somewhat tongue-tied.

I could not believe she knew my name but figured she might just have been told it.

When I first saw her, she didn't really look like I thought she was going to, like she would not particularly stand out in a crowd. Then as soon as she got made up, she looked incredible.

She was so lovely. Everything you read about her not being nice isn't true. She had so much time for everyone, from the make-up girls to the guy doing the lighting. She was really interested in my diving.

We got into the pool and were splashing each other. She tried to make it as normal as possible so it wasn't awkward. I kept wondering what I should talk to her about but she kept me chatting and laughing.

All the way through I was thinking of ways to ask her if I could take some pictures of her for my GCSE project. I particularly wanted one inspired by the original portrait by David Hockney. I was rehearsing it in my mind to make sure it didn't sound creepy. I had planned to say, 'Kate, I am doing a GCSE photography project. Would you be able to help with doing some photos?'

In the end I was like, 'Kate, can I take some photos of you, please?' I could hardly get the words out.

'Yeah, sure.'

Bruce Weber was happy – and wanted to take photos of me taking pictures of her. I felt really bad telling her what to do. In the end I said, 'To be honest I'm not going to tell you what to do because you know far more than I do.'

TONIA PRETENDING TO BE IN A HAIR AD IN ANOTHER ONE OF MY COURSEWORK PICTURES.

SHE WAS BRILLIANT AND IN ONE PHOTO BRUCE TOLD ME TO HOLD HER HAND, BECAUSE IT WOULD GIVE HIM AN EXCELLENT SHOT. WE DID ABOUT FIVE TO TEN MINUTES OF PHOTOS AND I FEATURED ONE PAGE OF THOSE PHOTOS IN MY COURSEWORK.

A couple of weeks later, the renowned photographer David Bailey also took some pictures of me for UK *Vogue* for a feature called 'Class of 2010', with other rising stars like actress Claudia Renton, campaigner Iris Andrews and model Alice Dellal. It felt quite strange suddenly being in a celebrity world that wasn't just about sport – but exciting and interesting too. It was also great being shot by David Bailey – it's what I used to call Dad when he took bad pictures!

The next week I had a few social events. This was a great chance to catch up with Nikita, Sophie and the gang. I went to my cousin Brooke's christening with my family and a few days later to Sophie's birthday meal, followed by Alex's sixteenth birthday party.

I really enjoyed the filming of *A Question of Sport* in London, which I did at the end of October. I do not really follow football but am more interested in the other Olympic sports and tennis. I was on Phil Tufnell's team along with Andy Cole. Our team won!

Around this time I also found out I would be sitting some of my GCSE exams early so was working very hard preparing for those. There was quite a big block of time for me to get some schoolwork under my belt before the end of the year.

Training-wise, I was also putting the time in as I was starting to learn my new dive, the twister – back two and a half somersaults, two and a half twists – which had a 3.6 tariff. It took me a long time to get it ready for competition. With every new dive, it's just a case of getting your

head round it. It felt like it needed so much energy to jump up to get all the moves in. We talked through it, visualized it, did it on the harness, off the lower boards, then upwards towards the 10m. There is lots of repetition and it's like piecing a puzzle together. I wanted to make sure I hammered it in. I knew I needed to do it slowly, as when I rush, there is much more potential for everything to go wrong.

I FELT SO NERVOUS IN TRAINING; I BECOME COMFORTABLE WITH ONE SET OF DIVES AND THEN HAVE TO PUSH MYSELF AGAIN. EVERY TIME I DO A DIFFERENT MOVE, IT'S LIKE TAKING A LEAP INTO THE UNKNOWN. BUT I TOLD MYSELF, AS I DO NOW, THAT THE SCHEMAS ARE ALL THERE WORKING. I HAD TO SWITCH OFF AND LET MY BODY DO IT.

Around then there was some stuff in the press about Laura Robson and me. I have never met her and it was the first time that the press had tried to pair me off with someone other than Tonia! I follow her on Twitter and she follows me, but I have never met her and normally see her when she is pulling loads of faces while playing, in the same way she has probably seen me gurning while diving. She said she was going to the Australian Open and I tweeted her saying, 'Good luck x'. And then all the newspapers said, 'He wrote good luck and signed off with a passionate kiss'! Doesn't everyone sign off with a kiss these days? I thought it was really funny.

In December I won BBC Young Sports Personality of the Year again, which was brilliant. It was the first year Burberry had dressed me so that felt pretty special, too. The tyre blew out on the way up to the

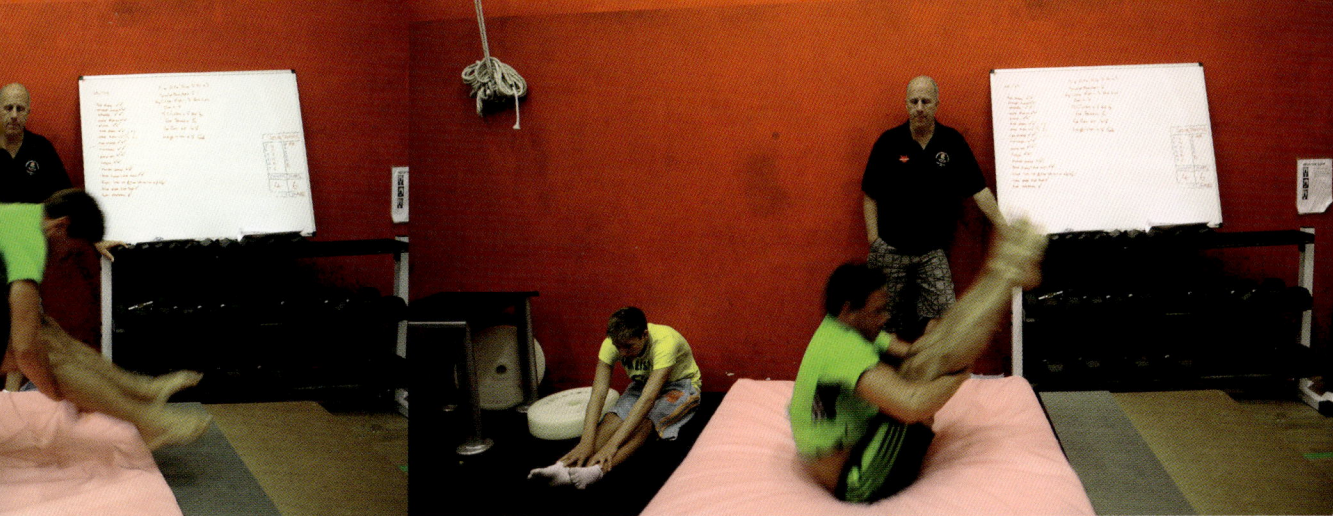

ceremony in Sheffield and we had to stop on the hard shoulder of the motorway. We were sat on the bank and I was really annoyed that we might miss the awards but the RAC rescued us in time. It is always amazing to go to ceremonies and meet the people you see on TV. If you are someone in sport you are there, so it was great to see everyone. Ellie Simmonds and Amir Khan gave me my award.

I also filmed a video for Sport Relief with James Corden. I'm a massive fan of *Gavin and Stacey* and he was starring as Smithy in a sketch in which he was nominated as 'coach of the year'. Part of the sketch was us doing a synchronized dive off the 10m board. When James took his clothes off and put his Speedos on, we did a belly bounce and everyone was laughing. He really does take the mick out of himself!

The first hurdle was getting him up onto the 10m platform; he was absolutely petrified. Initially he would not even jump off 3 metres and kept saying, 'I can't do it, I can't do it. I'm terrified.' After a good ten minutes, he jumped.

'I don't know how you keep doing it and keep doing it,' he said as we traipsed up 5m and then 7m, where he spent fifteen minutes on each board moaning about how high it was. Finally, he went straight up to the top board, where it took forty minutes for him to jump.

It was one take only – he refused to practise. He gave me a knowing look and we jumped. He screamed the whole way down and yelled:

'WHAT was that? You keep letting me down!' I found it so hard not to laugh, so I put my mouth just under the water to try and stop myself.

After our shoot he was asking about my diving and he suggested I start doing synchro with the Chinese as a sure-fire plan to get gold all the time. I had to explain that it does not work like that! He also asked me whether the Olympic Village was like university and a 'giant sex fest'. I told him I didn't know!

That year we spent Christmas at home. Our grandparents came over – it is all about the food and family. I love turkey but I hate Christmas pudding so I have chocolate yule log instead. We play games, watch TV and every year normally have a round of Play Your Cards Right. It starts with the youngest person, who puts a pound in the pot, and you could end up with £25 at the end.

2010 started with a roast dinner at my grandparents Rose and Dink's house and just a few days later it was back to school to face some mock and proper GCSE exams. I did mocks in English Literature and Physics and then sat the real GCSE Biology, Chemistry and Physics exams a few weeks later. In between these exams I opened a new leisure pool in Poole and did a diving session with James Cracknell, Olympic rowing champion, for the *Telegraph*. Again, they wanted a shot of us doing synchro off the top platform. After a few dives on the lower boards, we went up to 10m, and as James peered over the edge he said, 'There are two ways down: one hurts your ego and the other just hurts! I'm a lot taller than you. From where I'm standing, this is a 12m board.'

'Just push up on your toes and lean forwards,' I told him. I counted us in and we dived. It was weird doing a straight dive – it was like I had nothing to think about, rather than the normal thousand things. James slightly over-rotated and when the photographer asked if we could do it again, James gave him such a look that he said, 'I think I got it.' We all laughed.

In February I had my first competition of the year, the British Gas National Cup, which took place in Sheffield's Pond's Forge. I was the only diver ever to hold the titles of British, European and World Champion at the same time – and this was the first of the titles I needed to defend as well as the first time I did the twister in competition. It had gone well in training and I was pleased to be showcasing it in front of a home crowd but I had strained my shoulder, so wasn't on top form. Despite that, I taped it up to give it extra support and hoped for the best. Mum, Dad, William and Ben were in the audience, along with Grandma Rose, Grandma Jenny, Granddad Doug and Granddad Dink. My twister earned some 8s, which was great, but because I had been practising my harder dives so intensely, I had not been doing my older dives as much and I over-rotated my armstand back triple, piked. It takes a long time to get yourself in the right mental space to do a competition, and I think because I went back to some of my older list it confused me slightly. Pete dived brilliantly with seven perfect 10s en route to take the first place with 523.65 points. I finished in second with 483.60. I was really disappointed and frustrated with my silly mistakes but knew I had to take the positives away from it. Diving is an on-the-day sport – that's just the nature of it. It really gave me a kick up the backside.

I felt very deflated but talked to the team about whether we could name a diver who had successfully defended all their titles – or, indeed, anyone in any sport. So I had learned what it took to get to the top but also was learning what it was like to come back down again. The feeling of going in both directions was part of my experience, I guess, and I had to focus on the list of favourites – having fun and enjoying myself – and hope that the results would take care of themselves.

'IT IS ALWAYS JUST A CASE OF PRACTICE, PRACTICE AND MORE PRACTICE TO TRY AND DRILL IT DOWN. THE FRONT FOUR AND A HALF WAS THE LAST DIVE I MIGHT EVER HAVE TO LEARN OFF 10M, WHICH FELT STRANGE BUT MADE ME DETERMINED TO GET IT RIGHT. FOR A LONG TIME I DIDN'T THINK IT WOULD BE THE DIVE FOR ME.'

SETBACKS
AND
TRIUMPHS

AT A LOT OF MY BIG EVENTS, I WAS FOLLOWED BY THE BBC FILM CREW FOR THE DOCUMENTARY THEY WERE MAKING, 'THE DIVER AND HIS DAD'. THERE WERE JANE THE PRODUCER, THE SOUND MAN AND THE CAMERAMAN.

They also came to some sessions when I was learning the twister, took some footage of the family at home and planned to follow me through all my major competitions that year. I guess by then I had been under the spotlight for a while, and after the first few sessions forgot the cameras were there.

In February, Dad and I jetted to Abu Dhabi for the Laureus World Sports Awards, recognizing sportspeople around the world. I was nominated for the Laureus World Breakthrough of the Year Award along with F1 driver Jenson Button, cyclist Mark Cavendish, Argentinian tennis player Juan Martin del Potro, golfer Ji Yai Shin and German football club VfL Wolfsburg. It was really glamorous and there were so many amazing sports stars there. Jenson won the award – and when he collected his cup he said he's been around for ages, which made everyone giggle.

Dad and I were there for a few days and we were put up in the Emirates Palace, which was awesome. The building is a kilometre long if you walk from one end to the other and it has a private beach. During our stay, we got to be passengers in the F1 Yas Marina circuit car that sets the pace. It was great fun – we were really chucked around as we sped round the track. Dad was complaining that he could not walk, saying he felt sick! Hugh Grant was at the party but I didn't get the chance to say hello, though he came up to us at the airport when we were on our way home, shook my hand and told me to keep up the diving and that he would be watching in 2012.

Arriving home I picked up my GCSE results for my science exams and I got three A*s, which I was delighted with. I celebrated the following week at the Plymouth Diving Club Dinner and Dance, where everyone let their hair down and had fun outside a training environment.

Just a couple of days later I was on my way to Qingdao in China for the first of the FINA World Series events that year. I was delayed getting out there by a few days because my visa didn't go through in time. In this event I was doing my new dives and scored 520.35 but just missed out on a medal, finishing in fourth place. Sascha scored 541.50 to strike bronze behind Qiu Bo and Zhou Luxin in first and second place, respectively. I was still pleased because it was my best score of the year so far but it just made me realize that everyone else was pushing themselves harder and harder and that I needed to keep working on my new list to make sure I kept pace with them. It also meant that if I dropped one of my more difficult dives, because of my higher tariffs I would not be completely out of the running.

In February it was confirmed that Dad's cancer was back and the tumour was showing signs of regrowth. He had been going for regular scans to make sure everything was OK – and I knew that he'd been having some more panic attacks, so they had increased the steroids, but he didn't have any major symptoms that I knew about. I always thought it was a case of sorting out his medication and him getting well again and the tumour shrinking. I never for a million years thought it could beat him, you never think it will happen to your family. He still took me to training even when he was tired, and behaved just like normal, joking at every opportunity. When anyone asked him how he felt, he just said, 'About nineteen!' and then laughed. He said he wasn't in pain and tried his hardest to show William, Ben and me that he wasn't ill. I never, ever saw him complain or be miserable.

One day I went to see him have a scan – I told him he looked like Homer Simpson in the MRI machine. We played him some Beach Boys while the doctors were looking at the scans. I wanted to ask where the tumour was because I was interested but the pictures were flashing up so quickly and I could see that Grandma Rose was getting a bit upset, so I left it.

It was decided that rather than have another operation he would undergo a course of chemotherapy a few months later, which involved drugs through a drip and lots of tablets. I know now that they made him really sick but when he had it I was away for training camps and competitions, so I never saw him ill. On the phone he was always full of beans, telling me the news and what he had been doing.

When I was back in the UK, I did a photoshoot for our local newspaper with a young boy called Archie Barton. Archie is four years old and a few years ago he suffered from meningitis and lost both his legs and some fingers due to septicaemia. His parents have started a fundraising campaign called Archie's Story to help raise enough money to buy prosthetic legs for him. His mum saw my dad one day at the pool and told him about the appeal, and as soon as I heard about it I wanted to get on board and help. I wanted to do what I could to help raise awareness as I think it's very important to do what we can to help others. He is a lovely and very bubbly little boy and I took him to our local swimming pool. I'm just glad I can help in situations like this.

The next part of the World Series was in Veracruz in Mexico. This competition didn't go as well as I'd hoped and a few bad dives meant I didn't qualify for the final round. It was even more frustrating that the Sheffield part of the World Series was cancelled due to the volcanic ash cloud so we did the competition in Veracruz again as all the divers were there. I was in second place all the way through then missed one of my dives and finished in fourth place. It was disappointing but I was more determined to train and practise even harder for the next competition back at the pool at home. It did take us a long time to get back to Plymouth because of the ash cloud, as we had to go from Veracruz to Mexico City, then to Canada, Paris and finally London, which took three days of planes, trains and cars!

I was continuing to learn new dives – a back three and a half somersaults piked position and the front four and a half, which everyone was learning for the forthcoming competitions. It is always just a case of practice, practice and more practice to try and drill it down. The front four and a half was the last dive I might ever have to learn off 10m, which felt strange but made me determined to get it right. For a long time I didn't think it would be the dive for me.

It was a quieter couple of months, which gave me a chance to catch my breath and focus on school and training. I started May with two days of GCSE Photography exams. May is a busy month for family birthdays as we had my youngest brother Ben's eleventh birthday on the 12th, my sixteenth on the 21st and William's fourteenth on the 30th. On my big day, we had a party with my family and friends and my Aunty Marie made this amazing cake, which was a little man made of icing sugar on the top of a high platform. After I had blown my candles out I made him jump off the platform into the water, which was made of jelly. Sophie and Nikita bought me a goldfish, which I called Sikita after them.

My school friends, my brothers and I also went zorbing. It's basically where you roll down a hill in an orb, which is made of transparent plastic. It was like being in a hamster ball and definitely something completely different.

A few days later I was photographed by Bettina von Zwehl for a project with the National Portrait Gallery called 'Roads to 2012', a series of pictures of athletes, politicians and engineers and all the people working behind the scenes to make the London 2012 Olympics and Paralympics happen. She took the picture on Bovisand beach – Dad suggested it because it's my favourite beach and it's really hidden away and peaceful. Launching it I spoke about the inspirational people in my life, like Sir Steve Redgrave and Tanni Grey-Thompson.

It was Dad's fortieth birthday and we celebrated with a meal. We bought him a helicopter flying lesson, which he loved. Going out with him was always so amusing – at that time the World Cup was on so when we drove around he thought it was hilarious to blow his vuvuzela at random people out of the window.

In preparation for the Europeans, I was training for six hours a day.

One day I was training as normal and as I was taking off for a dive and getting into a tuck shape I got cramp in my boob and in my right hip flexor. I was spinning round but I could not stay tucked, because it was so painful, and I landed upright but I was loose in my back.

I really stung and was in agony. I had to pull out of the British Diving Championships in Sheffield at the end of June and did rehabilitation work and physiotherapy sessions twice a day. I still went to the competition to watch and have treatment, but I was annoyed because it meant that I missed my school prom. Thankfully, the work to repair the injury was a success and a few weeks later I was back training as normal again.

At the beginning of July, I did a Get Set Go Free Media Day for my sponsor Nestlé. My family and I went kite buggying for the day and were filmed and photographed. It was really good fun. The following week, I went to Silverstone to watch the British Grand Prix. It was a fantastic day and I got to meet Michael Schumacher.

Then I was busy preparing and training to head to Rome on 25 July. This was for a pre-camp before the European Championships, where I was hoping to defend the title. I was completely injury-free and everything was going well. On 8 August, we left Rome to go to the Budapest event. I was going to be away for seven weeks.

Two days before the event I was practising and as I brought my hands together, I missed and my arms were bent back behind my head really quickly. My tricep was in agony. I didn't know it had torn but it was so painful and each time they touched it in massage, I was in unbearable pain, so we rested it and iced it. I taped it up as much as I possibly could but I could barely lift it above my head. I was so annoyed but every time I moved, it was so sore.

At the hospital I had an ultrasound scan. I just wanted to find out what was wrong. The lady said she could not see anything and told me it was fine to dive. I didn't understand her diagnosis though – it still really hurt.

Arriving at the outdoor pool in Budapest, it was still so painful. Dad had delayed a course of chemotherapy to come and watch and Granddad Dink was there with him.

MY FIRST COMPETITION WAS THE SYNCHRO BUT AFTER THE PRELIMS WE MADE THE DECISION I NEEDED TO PULL OUT BECAUSE IT HURT SO MUCH AND I RISKED INJURING MYSELF FURTHER. I FELT SO DEFLATED AND FRUSTRATED THAT I WASN'T ABLE TO DEFEND MY EUROPEAN TITLE. I FELT LIKE THE SEASON WAS GOING AWFULLY. SASCHA KLEIN PICKED UP THE TITLE WITH 534.85 POINTS.

In the end, I just competed in the 3m springboard. This is not a discipline I train on very often and I made some errors on a couple of my dives, meaning I finished in ninth place. I had hoped to get a medal so it was a disheartening result and felt like it was a pretty rubbish end to the competition.

From there, we travelled straight to Singapore for the Youth Olympics and my arm had not got any better. Eventually, I had an MRI and it showed up a grade two tear on the part of the tricep that connects the ligament to the muscle. It was relief to know what was wrong but I had to pull out of the platform event again and the doctors told me just to see how it was from day to day.

By the time we arrived in Singapore, I had calmed down and knew how important it was to properly rehab my arm. I had such amazing help from the physios, Lucy and Amanda, who were brilliant and always

there for me. They devised lots of different programmes to get me back to full fitness. I was so frustrated but tried to tell myself that it was better that I had loads of injuries then rather than in 2011 or 2012. I still stuck with the team and we managed to do some fun stuff. One day we had a go on the surf simulator on the beach, which was harder than it looked. We also did some filming for Blue Peter at an infinity pool at the top of a hotel, where there was an incredible view.

Gradually my arm got stronger. The physios were amazing and one of them got up at 4 a.m. on the morning that we travelled to Tucson in Arizona for the Junior World Championships just so she could give me a treatment before we left.

I was the Senior World Champion and was hoping to do the double, but my injury prevented me from competing in my event yet again. I competed in the 3m and this time finished in sixth place. It is always gutting not to win a medal but if it had been a senior competition, because of the way the tariffs are worked out, I would have finished third. We still had a good time and outside the competition some of the GB team learnt a 'Waka Waka' dance and competed against the Americans in a 'dance-off', which was really funny.

I had to sit my GCSE exams during the build-up to all the summer competitions and on the day of my results I received the standard brown envelope. I was almost as nervous as in the big competitions – I really could not bear to rip it open and look. I had not done particularly well in my mocks so when I finally opened it and saw I had got four A*s and two As, I was over the moon. I pretended to Dad that I was really upset, and then delivered the good news. While my friends went out to party, I celebrated by going to training!

I decided I wanted to do Spanish, Maths and Photography for my A Levels. I always want to have something to fall back on and plan to go to university, while continuing my diving training.

We headed to Leeds for a training camp at the end of September before leaving for the Commonwealth Games in India on 5 October. All being well I would definitely be competing in the 10m platform individual event but it was still to be decided who was doing the synchro event. At that time, there were three divers – myself, Max Brick and Peter Waterfield – and it was down to Alexei Evangulov, Performance Director of British Diving, to decide which pairing would compete. Alexei had joined the previous year just after Steve Foley left to do a similar job in America.

While we were in Leeds, we worked hard but we also took time out to go to Alton Towers and to the cinema. Every day we went to the local shop to get some pic 'n' mix and a Fab lolly – it was our treat! There were worries about security in India but I wasn't concerned. It was reported that the organizers were 'on alert' following news that a Pakistan-based terror group was planning an attack on the games leading up to the closing ceremonies. Pete decided to stay at home because he has two children and everyone respected his decision, so Max and I were going to do the synchro together.

In my experience, every single international competition I go to is always so secure, especially inside the athletes' village, which is always protected with wire fences and metal gates at the entrance. I felt I needed to trust the team managers. I was also keen to go around Delhi with my camera, because I was working on a photography project entitled 'Urban'. When we arrived I was impressed: everything was clean, the security was tight and the food, very importantly, was great.

It was the first time I was going away without either of my parents coming along to cheer me on: Dad was in the middle of a course of chemo and Mum had just had a routine operation. I really missed Dad being there to joke and mess around with me, but I felt like it was a chance to prove to myself that I could perform without them there and I knew they would be glued to their televisions and phones.

My first competition was the synchro. We had only trained about nine times during the year because of my injuries, so we felt quite unpractised. We were still training as a trio with Pete and were both nervous. Warming up alongside Australians Matthew Mitcham and Ethan Warren, we knew they were definitely the team to beat. My tricep was still hurting but the adrenalin was flowing, so I didn't feel any pain. The nerves worked in our favour and it was the first time we had landed on our heads every time and we led from the second dive right through to the last. We were shaking before our last dive – the twister – because it was the dive that won Matt the Olympics, but we nailed it and I scored a personal best of 439.65, beating the Australians by more than 15 points. We were over the moon – and it was fantastic sharing the experience of being on the podium together when the National Anthem was being played.

Less than a minute later, I was on the phone home. I was convinced there was nothing that Dad could do to embarrass me – after all, he was at home on the sofa, right. Wrong – I did a radio interview and there he was singing, 'Olé, olé, olé, olé!' He later told me that he was going to sing 'Give Me Oil in My Lamp' because he used to say that me and my brothers are the oil in his lamp, but he forgot what he was supposed to be singing.

We went back to the hotel delighted and I treated myself to a bit of ice cream. I had to get my head down and get some rest but I was exhausted and dropped off immediately.

That night my documentary 'The Diver and His Dad' aired on BBC1. I hadn't seen it – Dad had been down to London to give it his seal of approval. It was then that his illness came back out in the media. People realized his tumour had got worse again. I didn't mind people knowing but I didn't want anyone bothering him. When I watched it I was pleased with it because it was completely genuine. The moment when he had put a ladder outside the house and popped his head up past my window as I was checking out my new room was just how it happened. I was starting to disturb Ben in the evenings so we decided I needed my own space. In my room I have a huge king Vi-Spring bed with a patriotic Union Jack bed cover, a desk, a big TV on the wall and loads of pictures of holidays and diving events decorating the wall. Dad used to tease me, telling me he and Mum watched my TV when I was away because it is so much bigger than the one in the front room.

IN THE DOCUMENTARY, WHEN HE TALKED ABOUT MAYBE NOT SEEING HIS GRANDCHILDREN OR 2012, I JUST THOUGHT HE WOULD. I DIDN'T QUESTION IT. I THOUGHT HE WAS INVINCIBLE.

Going into the individual competition at the Commonwealth Games, I felt more relaxed with a gold medal already under my belt. There were eleven of us taking part but I knew again that Matt would be my competition that day – he was coming in on top form, while I still didn't feel like I was firing on all cylinders. It was obvious when we were training in the run-up it would be a battle of nerves. It felt like more of a psychological battle.

After coming second in the semis, I was diving first, which is a good position to be in, because I could put pressure on him, a tactic that I was getting used to using to my advantage, as I had done in Rome.

'GOING INTO THE INDIVIDUAL COMPETITION AT THE COMMONWEALTH GAMES, I FELT MORE RELAXED WITH A GOLD MEDAL ALREADY UNDER MY BELT.'

ALEXEI TOLD ME I SHOULD BE HAPPY WITH A MEDAL BUT I TOLD HIM I WAS AFTER THE GOLD. I NEEDED IT TO PROVE TO MYSELF I STILL HAD IT; I COULD STILL WIN A COMPETITION AFTER THE YEAR OF SETBACKS AND INJURIES. I KNEW I HAD IT IN ME.

After my first two dives, my back two and a half somersaults, two and a half twists, and forward three and a half, Matt was in the lead, but on my third dive – an inward three and a half somersaults with tuck, which I normally struggle with – I earned straight perfect 10s, only the second time I have managed it during my career. I punched the air with both hands as a huge cheer filled the stadium. Matt, who was preparing to dive after me, applauded as my scores flashed across the screen. And after his next dive, he maintained his lead with no less than 9.5s. In the fourth round, I re-took the lead with my armstand back triple somersault – and narrowly extended it again in my fifth dive, the back three and a half somersaults with tuck, to 1.75 points.

But it was all down to the final dive. I peered over the edge, breathing slowly and tipped off the board to take reverse three and a half somersaults. It was a ripped entry with barely a splash – it was good.

Matt then took the crucial dive, his hardest dive – back two and a half somersaults with two and a half twists, with a higher tariff than mine. He needed an average score of 8.9 to win. I stood by, watching and waiting.

He looked up for inspiration, prepared himself, then leapt. The splash told its own story and everyone had started cheering before his scores – ranging from 5.5 to 7 – came up. I was hugging my coaches.

On the podium, Matt jokingly grabbed my medal and put it up against himself, which was amusing. Loads of things were going through my head as I stood there. I replayed the dives in my head and then thought back to the hard times and all the hard work I'd put in to be there, with the Union Jack above my head and the National Anthem playing. It felt like a huge journey with so much work and so many sacrifices along the way but I was on the top block, where I wanted to be.

After an awful year riddled with injury it was an incredible result – it felt like everything came right again. I was delighted. I called Dad immediately and he was equally thrilled for me.

My first day back in England was pretty hectic with a full day of media interviews, including *Sky News*, *BBC Breakfast* and *Daybreak*. After a long day I headed home to Plymouth to see my family and show them my medals. They were so proud of my achievement.

THE CANCER BATTLE

A few days later my family and I went to Disneyland in Paris for three days. We were not able go anywhere outside the EU because of Dad's illness – his chemotherapy meant he could get a blood clot if he flew so we knew that nowhere would be really hot because of the time of year. He had promised us a holiday, though, and my brothers, Mum and I love rollercoasters, so the obvious choice was Disneyland. I always feel I have to act so grown up when I am diving and doing interviews, so it was really good to be able to let my hair down and act like a big kid. We made sure we had a family picture with Mickey Mouse, who also did some diving impressions, and we generally larked around. At the airport we were messing around and put Dad into a wheelchair, and I joked that we were like Andy and Lou from *Little Britain*. I locked him in the disabled loo for a while, too!

Then on 10 November I did *A Question of Sport on Tour* when it came to Plymouth at The Pavilions. I was on the panel with Matt Dawson and

Andrew Castle. There was this really embarrassing moment when Matt asked about a mark on my face and I said, 'It's a carpet burn!' – and then Matt buzzed his buzzer before doing an impression of someone rubbing their head against the carpet! Everyone fell about laughing but it was actually from coming down the stairs in a sleeping bag racing the synchronized swimmers. I fell out and got a horrible burn on my arm and head. I actually said it was with my brothers. I cannot imagine what he would have thought if I fessed up that it was me and a bunch of synchro girls!

I am a patron of the Samantha Dixon Brain Tumour Trust and attended their fundraising ball to help raise as much money as we could in November. Mum and Dad and my grandparents were there and everyone got really dressed up in black tie. Samantha was diagnosed with brain cancer when she fourteen and died a few days before her seventeenth birthday in 1996. Her parents, Neil and Angela Dickson, have been campaigning ever since to raise awareness and feel that research into brain cancer is underfunded, despite it being the biggest killer of people under forty, and it has grown to become the UK's biggest brain tumour charity. They asked me to become a patron and I was more than happy after my experience of Dad's illness, as it is very close to my heart. I am really proud to be part of the great work they are doing, because there needs to be more research into this horrible disease.

In December there was a raft of award shows. First up was the BBC Teen Awards, where I won the Sporting Hero Award and I met stars such as Ellie Goulding, Pixie Lott and the guys from *The Inbetweeners*. The girls were screaming so loud, I thought I needed ear plugs! I tried to meet Katy Perry but she was hiding in her dressing room, though bizarrely in the Green Room I spent ages chatting to Russell Brand's cousin, before I realized he was related to Russ. We stayed at the

Dorchester, which was really posh and old. To be honest, I'm just as happy in a Premier Inn!

I also got screamed at the T4 Stars of 2010 – it was crazy. When they showed a picture of me in my trunks, I thought that it might blow my eardrums. It's weird because I do not think of myself as some sort of pin-up. I look the way I do because of my sport. It feels good to be moving into the showbiz side of things, as well as sport. It's just something different – and always interesting, although I don't think it's quite as glamorous as lots of people think.

I am a massive fan of *The X Factor* and I was very excited to go to one of the live shows a week later. I met all the finalists, although I was gutted not to meet Cheryl Cole as I am a big fan of hers. But I did meet Simon, who was coming down the corridoor backstage and then stopped and said, 'Hi, Tom. You're the diver, aren't you?' and shook my hand. I was so surprised he knew who I was!

THEN WE SAW LOUIS AND HE WAS TELLING ME I SHOULD JOIN A BOYBAND LIKE ONE DIRECTION.

'CAN YOU SING?'

'ER, NO.'

'DANCE?'

'ER, NOT REALLY.'

'WELL YOU CAN JUST BE AT THE BACK AND LOOK GOOD!'

MAYBE I'LL THINK ABOUT IT IF THE DIVING GOES WRONG . . .

The biggest diva there was Wagner. He seemed a bit weird – he strutted around arrogantly and Cher was totally caked in make-up, while Katy was skipping around. Sitting in the audience was completely different to watching it on the TV.

December was another busy month with the build-up to Christmas. At the start of the month I did some filming for *A Question of Sport* as the mystery guest where I went round Plymouth Christmas Market.

I was meant to be in a competition on 3 December but this was cancelled due to the snow. It meant I could go to my college awards, where I won for photography and sport.

It was a week of awards as on the 6th I won the *Plymouth Herald* Young Sports Personality of the Year, on the 15th the local BBC Young Sports Personality of the Year, and on the 19th the overall BBC Young Sports Personality of the Year for the third time. It was a real shock as I had won it twice in a row so I didn't think they would give it to me for a third time. It was an amazing evening and I got to see an idol of mine, David Beckham, who won the Lifetime Achievement Award and he and Victoria were sat a few rows in front of us. He gave me a wink as I was going up on stage, which was cool, but unfortunately I didn't get to meet him because he and Victoria came in really late and snuck out first. Everyone clapped him so much that my hands were a bit sore afterwards! Dad kept saying, 'What do you mean, did we meet the Beckhams? Surely you mean to say, did the Beckhams meet us?'

I was really scared getting up in front of so many people – I always start really nervous, then get into it and it's fine.

As part of my work with the *Daily Mail* I had a tour of the Olympic site the week before Christmas to help mark the fifth anniversary of the group. Like a proper sightseer, I took my camera to take some snaps. The Aquatics Centre, designed by British-Iraqi Zaha Hadid, was a maze of scaffolding and diggers underneath the shark-style roof, but was unrecognizable since the last time, and was all on schedule. I was ushered up the wooden ladders and through some yellow doors to pose for Andy Hooper on the 5m board in my hard hat. The platforms are incredible and unlike anything anyone has ever seen before. They are made from high-tech self-compacting concrete poured into glass-fibre-reinforced moulds with a core of steel bars. They look like a wave coming out of the floor. We also inspected the blue and white tiling at the bottom of the swimming pool, where it will be possible to alter the floor depth. The visit really spurred me on to train harder. I can't wait for 2012.

It was then Christmas and I had a fantastic time celebrating with my family. Dad dressed up as Santa as usual and we messed around in the snow. On Christmas Day we went out for a meal, which was good, but it just wasn't the same as eating a Christmas dinner at home. My best present was a soup-maker. It sounds funny but I make soup quite a lot, as it's a quick and healthy snack I can make when I get back from training in the evenings.

My first day back to training was the 29th after four days of lying around, eating and relaxing at home. I did miss it though and I always feel re-energised after a break. I hadn't trained with Pete or Max for a while, so we got together in Leeds to get some time in.

ON NEW YEAR'S DAY, IT WAS ANOTHER FAMILY GET-TOGETHER AFTER I HAD A BIT OF A LIE-IN. IT FELT REALLY WEIRD THINKING THAT THE OLYMPICS WERE 'NEXT YEAR'. IT SEEMED TO BE COMING ROUND REALLY QUICKLY.

In January, I started diving with Pete as Alexei searched for the most competitive team for 2012. In training together, we focused mainly on our timing – it's not just about getting it right yourself but making sure you are totally in time with your partner. I'm slightly taller than Pete and have longer legs so I have to do a longer run-up on the front four and a half, for example. He would count us in on all the other dives but because he was in front on that one, we had to swap so I was counting. In Plymouth and Southampton, where we train, the seating area is too low to video takeoffs, so Leeds was the best place because it allows us to film our dives, watch them on playback and break everything down. By the end of our sessions both Andy, and Pete's coach, Lindsey Fraser, were pleased with our progress and our form in the air.

Our first synchro event together was at the British Gas National Cup in Southend. Pete has always been someone who I have looked up to and there is always a bit of healthy competition between us, so we are constantly on each other's tails during individual performances.

Judges always like it when there is a World Champion and an Olympic silver medallist diving together because they are expecting to give higher scores. We had a higher degree of difficulty than any other partnership – and included the front four and a half for the first time, which we executed well. We won gold with 438.54, which was only five points off what Max and I had got at the Commonwealths, so it was a good result. Dad was in the crowd, videoing us as usual.

I practise springboard once a week and did the competition for a bit of fun and variety. I went out there and got a silver medal and a score that qualified me for the senior circuit on springboard, which was a bit of a surprise.

Pete edged me into second place in the platform event the next day. We both dived quite badly – I finished on 472 points, to Pete's 494. Max was in third with 399. I find it hard to motivate myself at national competitions because there's not the same adrenalin rush as there is on the international stage. I was also using all my new dives on the list for the first time ever. Pete's list was slightly easier and he landed on his head more, while I was still getting my new dives consistent. I was finding that my front four and a half was getting easier. When I first learnt it

PETE HAS ALWAYS BEEN
SOMEONE WHO I HAVE
LOOKED UP TO AND THERE
IS ALWAYS A BIT OF HEALTHY
COMPETITION BETWEEN US,
SO WE ARE CONSTANTLY ON
EACH OTHER'S TAILS DURING
INDIVIDUAL PERFORMANCES

I thought it really wasn't going to be my dive, but the more I practised it in competition, the better it was getting.

The day before the event, Dad had gone into hospital for a routine check-up with his doctor before I left and was told he had another tumour at the back of his head. He didn't tell me until I got home. I had asked him and Mum at the event how they had got on and they kept saying 'we'll talk about it later'. Apparently there was a journalist nearby and obviously they wanted to tell me in private but at the time I couldn't understand as I thought it would be the normal routine check and the existing tumour would be shrinking. It was a real shock.

Then a couple of days later Dad was driving the van and we hit a row of parked stationary cars, writing off our van in the process. He blamed being dazzled by the sun as he came round the corner, and while it was pretty scary, no one was hurt so I thought nothing more of it.

A week later he woke up with terrible pain in his head. He and Mum thought it was just a headache and didn't think it was anything to do with the new tumour. They called the hospital and they told him to go straight in. Mum woke me up to tell me because it was so early, but when I got up an hour later, they had still not left because he was finding it so hard to move.

He deteriorated really quickly and within three days he lost all the movement on the left side of his body. He would get into the bath and not be able to get out and then when he stood up he would collapse to the floor. It was terrifying because it was the first time we had seen the symptoms of his cancer. He could not stand up, move his fingers or feel anything on the left side. He kept falling over. I didn't really talk to anyone about it apart from my mum. If I spoke to my grandparents, they got quite emotional, so I just asked Mum lots of questions. I had told her I wanted to know exactly what was happening. I thought I could handle it and help my brothers, too. Of course I was upset and scared but I thought it was a case of getting over it with some help and the right drugs.

The new tumour was putting pressure on the part of the brain that controls movement and the doctors pumped him full of steroids to reduce the swelling. It looked like he had had a stroke but as the swelling went down he slowly started to regain, with help from the physios, some of the movement he had lost. After about a week he still couldn't move his left hand – he was so frustrated and despite doing everything he could, it still remained by his side.

One day, when my little cousin Brooke went to see him and said, 'Hello, Uncle Robert,' he started waving. It was a reflex – but a monumental step. Both he and the doctors were amazed and delighted at the progress. From then on he waved at everyone on the ward. He was determined to get through it.

For a while he was in a wheelchair and I pushed him around hospital with William and Ben. There were more *Little Britain* Andy and Lou jokes; we kept saying he would pull a moony if we looked away.

They told him he would not walk again, which was devastating for everyone, but he was determined. Towards the end of the stay, the physios were trying to get him to walk with a Zimmer frame – and he said that was absolutely terrifying but if I could do what I did every day, he would do it. He didn't change and was still joking with the nurses, who were so helpful and lovely.

It was really anxious but I didn't allow myself to start worrying that he would not get better. Mum and Dad insisted that everything remained exactly the same, so we all went to school as normal and then training, while Ben and William continued with their rugby. On Valentine's Day after training, Tonia and Brooke came over for a meal. Tonia's boyfriend was away because he is in the Army and Brooke was single, so Mum cooked us fajitas and the three of us and Mum had dinner by candlelight!

Everyone always wants to know if I have a girlfriend, but I'm single at the moment. I was seeing a synchronized swimmer at the start of 2011 but she lived in Bristol and I wasn't driving, so it didn't really happen. I also have a bit of a soft spot for an American diver, Kassidy. I always look forward to seeing her and spending time with her when we're away together but it would never work out properly because she lives in Texas. I don't think I'll have a proper girlfriend for a while because I go away so much. It's always really complicated.

Dad was staying positive and always saying there are people worse off, like troops in Afghanistan. Thankfully the tumour stopped growing and he went on a new chemotherapy drug for five days every four weeks. The new medicine, temozolomide, didn't make him as sick as the last chemo drug he took.

I had to go away to Russia for three weeks just before he came home from hospital. It was difficult and I didn't want to leave but I knew he was being discharged, which made it easier. I spoke to him as much as I could while I was away and he always put the best side forward. We would do FaceTime on our iPhones and he would always show me how he was walking and do stupid dancing to make me laugh. He would annoy Mum by getting on the bus in to town by himself and joke about it when he got home. The doctors could not believe the progress he made.

IT WAS FREEZING IN PENZA – EVERY TIME YOU WENT OUTSIDE YOUR BOGIES FROZE! I COMPETED IN THE SPRINGBOARD AND WON SEVENTH IN MY FIRST EVER SENIOR INTERNATIONAL. IT'S A VERY DIFFERENT DISCIPLINE AND MUCH MORE ABOUT STRENGTH.

In the 10m, I put all my new dives together. My front four and a half was good, which was a bonus, but my other dives, like my armstand, were inconsistent and not quite there. I came fourth with a score of 465. I felt my performance was in a bit of a valley but tried not to worry.

During the women's synchro competition, one of the British divers, Monique Gladding, who was diving with Megan Sylvester, struck her head during her inward three and a half tuck dive. She hit it with a thwack, was knocked unconscious, and fell through the air like a ragdoll. It was savage. Nick Robinson-Baker, Monique's husband Steve and the Russian coach dived to the bottom of the pool to rescue her but she had been under for about twenty seconds. Megan was looking around stunned – it was horrible. Blood was all over the poolside.

She was resuscitated while we were all sat there and was whisked off in an ambulance. Only two people have been killed by diving during the whole history of the sport. The only dive you can do it on is the reverse three and a half and you hit the back of your neck, breaking it instantly.

Thankfully, we found out soon after that she was OK, bar whiplash and a nasty gash on the top of her head, but the whole episode was horrifying.

Two weeks later, 350 miles north-west of Penza, we were competing at the first leg of the FINA Series in Moscow, in the pool that they dived in for the Olympics in 1980. We didn't compete in the synchro because Pete was struck down by a cold. However, I did get a place in the final of the 10m after performing a great front four and a half in the semis. I scored well on my first three dives and was in third place but missed my entry on my front four and a half, so finished in fifth with 459.20. Again, it wasn't a great score but I wasn't too concerned and knew I needed to keep improving my new dives.

Back home my Comic Relief sketch was on the TV, the one where I sat next to Richard Madeley and Sebastian Coe. Sadly not everyone was there when I filmed my bit but it was great fun. James Corden was hilarious again; I had to try so hard to stop myself laughing. It raised an amazing £74m too, which is incredible.

When I was home I also had a meeting with Madame Tussaud's about doing a waxwork. They came down to Plymouth and brought some photos of me in different poses to see which one I thought we should do and what face I would normally make when I was diving. I just held the position they wanted and they stood me on a turntable and took sixteen photos from all different angles. After drawing lots of dots all over me, they measured from point to point. They took a mould of my

teeth and my hands and matched up my skin and hair colour and had all these eyeballs so they could match up the right eye colour. The fake eyeballs were gross!

The second leg of the FINA Series was in Beijing. The Bird's Nest was just how I remembered it from the Olympics. Pete and I performed in our first international together and got a 10 for our reverse three and a half somersaults with tuck, which showed we were starting to gel more. We won the bronze and scored a personal best of 459.87, just pipped to silver by the Germans, who scored a tiny 0.03 more than us.

Frustratingly, in the individual event, I failed to reach the final because my new dives were not sharp enough. It was good to be back in Beijing and we visited the Great Wall of China with all the team. It was really steep, about 300 steps, but worth it when we got to the top. I took some photos and admired the views.

HOWEVER, AT THE BACK OF MY MIND I WAS ALWAYS THINKING ABOUT DAD. I KNEW HE WAS FIGHTING THE BIGGEST BATTLE OF HIS LIFE.

LOSING
DAD

Things with Dad weren't good and after impressing the doctors by walking, he started to go backwards again. He came to see me in the third leg of the FINA Series at Sheffield's Pond's Forge in April. He didn't think he would make it because it was such a long journey. He was also trying his hardest not to be in a wheelchair and insisted on trying to walk. Mum, Dad and my brothers left early on the Friday and made the 300-mile, six-hour trip to Sheffield and when I went to see him in the gallery, he was in floods of tears. It was really emotional – I'd never normally be allowed out to see my family before a competition, especially when tension was running high, but everyone knew I needed to be there. He was wearing his 'Give Me Oil in My Lamp' T-shirt. I don't think he ever knew that it would be his last competition and how ill he was. No one told him what the cancer might do because they never wanted him to give up. In the end he did go in the wheelchair. All it would have taken would be for one person to knock him slightly and he would have fallen over.

Being in front of a home crowd always feels amazing and Pete and I won gold with 449.43 points. We missed the first couple of dives but were in fourth place and continued to perform consistently well on our higher-tariff dives, and scored 8s and 9s on our front four and a half to move ahead of the Chinese duo, Yuan Cao and Yanquang Zhang. We never thought we would do it, so we were over the moon. Scoring 92.88 on our final dive, the back two and a half somersaults, two and a half twists, piked, we held the lead and the Chinese felt under pressure and failed to score highly. It was a brilliant feeling to know that our partnership was improving every time we competed although we still felt like we had lots of work to do. Dad was waving his flag and happy. It was a brilliant day.

On the second day, I scored my season's personal best in the 10m platform event with a score of 507.35, but I was just outside the medals after making an error on my armstand back triple somersaults piked for 5s and 5.5s, which dropped me down the leaderboard. I clawed some positions back with my final dives with the support of the home crowd, but I was unable to regain a medal position and finished fourth.

I went straight off to Guanajuato in Mexico after Sheffield without returning home. After finishing the synchro in fifth place, I qualified for the individual final in second place and was determined to do well. I was rewarded with a perfect ten for my front four and a half and a score of 105, which gave me the biggest score of the final. I also got 9.5s for my back three and a half, which was the best I had done internationally, and I was really pleased that I had performed my new list of dives really well and finished on a score of 562.80, a new British record. Qiu still took gold with 582.80 but I was delighted with my silver medal. The Chinese feel so far ahead of everyone that they can only chuck away gold when it comes to 2012. I know my list of dives is now the joint hardest but there is a fear that they could wheel out yet another Chinese diver doing some insane list. It feels like keeping up with the competition is really tough. Everyone is seriously whacking out massive degrees of difficulty.

And the difference is also in our training – while I maybe average around thirty-five dives from 10m per week, maybe ramping up to fifty dives before a big competition, Qiu will be doing 150 dives. It doesn't matter if he gets injured because there are ten other very good divers waiting to go in his place.

From Guanajuato we went to a three-day training camp at an outdoor pool at Guadalajara, before we were due to travel to Fort Lauderdale. It was in Guadalajara that Mum called.

ABOVE

When I left Mexico the others made a paper cut-out of me and took it with them everywhere.

'You need to come home, Tom,' she said.

'But why? I don't understand. We're in the middle of the competition, Mum. I can't just can't leave.'

I never realized that we could lose him but I knew it must be serious because I know how much he would have hated for me to be called home from a diving event. She told me they had booked a flight and I needed to be at the airport in an hour.

'You need to, Tom. Your Dad, he's not got long left.' she told me.

I swallowed hard. 'How long has he got?'

'They don't know if he'll last days, hours, maybe a week.'

'I'm coming,' I told her. I felt completely numb and unable to comprehend what she had told me. I couldn't believe it was happening. Part of me still felt he would pick himself up again. He'd made light of it for so many years and fought so hard and defied the doctors so many times.

The journey seemed to drag on forever. I'd look at my watch constantly, feeling that hours must have passed only to realize it was only ten minutes since I had last looked. I wished I'd never gone away. I was terrified I might be too late.

Within twenty-four hours I was home; Dad was in a bed in the front room and I saw just how ill he was. All my family – grandparents, aunts and uncles – were round the bed. He couldn't do anything and was struggling to keep his eyes open. He had a driver in each arm feeding drugs into his system and he seemed unaware of what was going on. I was really shocked and felt very emotional. When he saw me he punched a fist in the air, as if to say he was determined not to be defeated.

But the atmosphere had changed. All my family were there but everyone would have to go to the kitchen at regular intervals for a cry; to try and not show him how upset they were. I just didn't know what to do. It was horrible. By that point he had not drunk anything for about three days or eaten for five days. Mum kept saying to my brothers that he was 'really poorly' and that we needed to spend as much time with him as we could.

We sat down with William and Ben and she kept saying how poorly he was.

'YEAH I KNOW, HE'S ALWAYS BEEN REALLY POORLY,' BEN SAID. FOR AS LONG AS HE COULD REMEMBER, DAD HAD BEEN IN AND OUT OF HOSPITAL. HE PRESUMED THAT HE WOULD HAVE SOME DRUGS AND GET BETTER. HE DIDN'T UNDERSTAND.

'No, this time he's really poorly … He could die, Ben,' I whispered.

I felt I had to say it. Maybe it was too difficult for Mum to find the words.

That's when Ben dissolved into tears and we all started crying, trying somehow to comfort each other.

Nurses from Marie Curie and St Luke's Hospice were coming in twice a day. I asked when the next round of chemo pills was and was told that he was too weak to have any more. I kept thinking, 'What happens now?'

They were giving him medication to reduce the swelling but the more steroids they gave him the weaker he got, so they were trying to find a balance. They were giving him morphine to reduce the pain but it made him confused. He didn't know where he was. At one point he thought he was in the front seat of the BMW, which had been moved into the front room, three floors up. He used to get really angry about not being at home. It was very difficult. We tried to explain to him, but ultimately we knew it was the drugs that were making him disorientated.

The following day he seemed a bit better and more lucid. Sitting on his bed I asked him if he wanted a sip of water and he did, so I syringed some into his mouth, and patiently waited for him to swallow. Later in the day, he was asking for McDonald's and we rushed to get one and he ate it. Then he started to eat walnut cake and strawberry fool and he seemed to get better again. He helped me with my driving theory test revision, helping me memorize the answers to some of the questions, and was interested in training, asking which dives I had been practising.

I continued to train as normal and tried hard when I was diving not to think about Dad. Whenever I was at home I would sit by his bed and talk to him and tell him what I was doing. Often I didn't know whether he had heard me because it would take him about five minutes to reply, but I was patient and he always responded, even if it was a flicker of an eye or a brief smile.

After about two weeks, he went back downhill again and stopped eating and drinking. It was then that the doctors said he had hours or days, but then he asked for a McDonald's again and he seemed to get better. I still thought he could beat it, I still didn't think he was going to die. Each time he seemed to recover slightly, everyone was like 'Rob, you're just having us on!'

My family were still in and out of the house every day spending as much time as possible with him. I don't think he knew how long he was in the bed for but he was unable to do anything for himself. My mum was amazing and every time he messed himself she would clean him up and I would help her by rolling him over. It was hard; you never think that you are going to have to do that for your dad.

On my birthday I had my first driving lesson with my instructor, who was one of the diving parents. Dad wanted to get out of bed to watch me.

'Just put the sides down so I can hop out and run up the drive,' he said.

NO ONE WANTED TO SAY NO, SO WE PUT THE METAL BEDSIDES DOWN. HE TRIED SO HARD TO GET HIMSELF UP – DETERMINATION WAS ETCHED IN EVERY CREASE IN HIS FACE – BUT, OF COURSE, HE COULDN'T. HIS LEGS JUST WOULD NOT MOVE FOR HIM. TEARS STARTED ROLLING DOWN HIS FACE AND HE BEGAN TO GET ANGRY.

'PUT THE BED OUTSIDE! CARRY ME OUT! I WANT TO SEE TOM DRIVING.'

I felt so sad; it felt like it was almost a bigger deal for him than it was for me. It was a shame for him.

My lesson went well, and when I got back my Aunty Marie had made me a cake with L plates on the top in white and red icing. We showed it to Dad, who smiled and ate a slice.

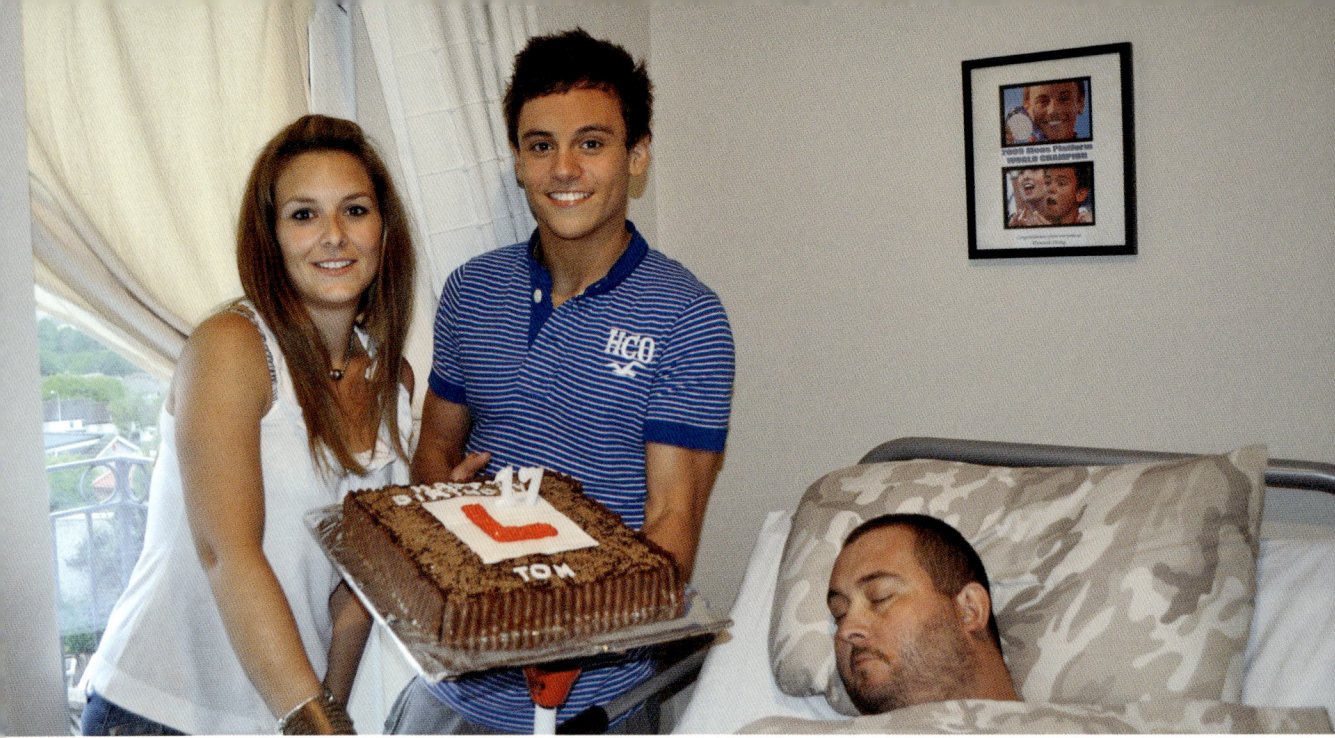

A few days later my new black Mini arrived from BMW, but we didn't tell him because we knew he would have wanted to come out and see it and he would not have been able to. It was just easier and less painful for everyone. That week I was on study leave, which made it a bit easier because I was at home. And, of course, I was really delighted with my new set of wheels and was looking forward to the freedom it would give me to travel around, especially to training every day, as Mum was doing everything for everyone: ferrying us about, cooking, cleaning and looking after Dad. Some of my friends like Sophie had already passed their tests, so I was keen to get mine under my belt as soon as I could.

Early on the Friday morning, Mum called my brothers and me downstairs in a panic. Dad was struggling to breathe. He had the oxygen mask on but his breathing sounded really wheezy and laboured. Mum told us to run down the road to get one of our neighbours who is a nurse and had looked after Dad in hospital. She rushed up to the house with us and gave him the asthma drug Ventolin, which he had been taking for a while. Thankfully, it seemed to help.

I went to training as normal but I was all over the place and could not concentrate on what I was doing. I got about halfway through the sessions and told Andy I wasn't able to do it. I was on my way back to the house when Mum called me to tell me that she thought I needed to come home.

When I arrived back at the house everyone was round Dad's bed. I could tell he was exhausted – his eyes were watering because he was putting so much effort into breathing. The doctors said he had hours but I still felt we had been there before. He could pull through; he was strong.

But this time was different and I think, deep down, I knew it. Each breath came ten seconds apart, then twelve seconds, then twenty seconds, then twenty-five seconds, then thirty seconds.

We all whispered our goodbyes to him while we thought he could hear us. It was incredibly emotional – I told him how much I loved him and thanked him for everything he had done for me. Periodically, his breathing would pick up and then become stretched out again. I didn't want to leave him and held his hand the entire time. I have a large cuddly monkey and he managed one final hug.

At about 9 p.m. we decided to take the oxygen mask off. The doctor told us it would not make any difference and Dad hated it being on his face.

Then it felt like a waiting game, it was awful. We were taking his heart rate and at one stage it reached 180 beats per minute. The doctor said it would have been the equivalent of running a marathon. His oxygen levels were a third of the amount they should have been and he was breathing really fast. I was holding his hand and told him to squeeze my hand.

I was willing him on and was telling him, 'Come on, Dad. You can get through this, I know you can.' He fingers closed around my hand and I felt the smallest amount of pressure.

He could still hear me and I didn't want to let go.

Soon after, he fell unconscious and his breathing slowed down again and he would make us all jump when he did take a breath. Everyone was in the room – Mum, William, Ben, both sets of grandparents, my Aunty Marie and Uncle Jamie, and their families. We all had our sleeping bags and planned to sleep in the room with him.

Eventually his breathing slowed and slowed and the inhalations were coming so far apart until they finally just stopped.

Everyone started crying – I just looked at him and could not believe it. I was like, 'What? Is that it?'

I sat holding his hand for the next half an hour. As the tears ran down my face, I stroked his head. He just looked like he was sleeping. After a while I took his hand from under the cover where I was holding it. His skin was completely white and his nails and veins were so pale they were hard to see; I could not get my head around the fact that there wasn't any blood running through his arms. It didn't make sense.

I let go of his hand and gave him one final hug, feeling his once strong body in my arms. The nurses had arrived and did the final checks. We wrapped him in his favourite Union Jack blanket so he would not get cold.

I went into the kitchen and sobbed with everyone else.

It's like time had stopped but a while afterwards, back in the front room, I leant over to give him one final kiss. His head felt cold on my lips.

I walked away. I know the undertakers came and carried him out on a stretcher but I didn't want to see that; see the last time he would ever be in our home. The place he was always laughing, joking, making us breakfast, helping us with our homework. It didn't seem real.

I found out that in 2006 he was told that he maybe had months or perhaps a year at the most to live and he kept exceeding everyone's expectations. It was almost like his personality could beat it.

At about 3 a.m., we all went to bed. Ben went in with Mum and my Grandma Jenny and Granddad Doug stayed too. Lying in bed, I tossed and turned as a million thoughts were whirring round my head: How can I not have my dad here? How come my dad will never see 2012? He's never going to see my A-Level results. He's never going to meet my children. Why us? I thought about everything I had done, every podium I had stood on with Dad looking on crying, every training session I had been to and Dad was there in the balcony talking to the other parents, clapping each dive I made. Hundreds of thousands of them and he clapped every one. I thought about everything I want to do and to achieve and the fact he would never see it. It felt so unfair.

Waking up in the morning, my first thought was that it was a normal Saturday and I needed to go training and then I remembered and I felt terrible beyond words.

The news was released to the media and there was a real outpouring of condolences on Twitter and Facebook. Then the flowers started arriving. The house looked like a florist's – even McDonald's sent a massive bouquet. We had hundreds of letters and cards, including ones from the Prime Minister and Seb Coe. It didn't make it any easier, but it felt good to hear how many people he had touched. It seemed like the nation was as shocked as we were.

It was important that we had stuff to focus on. Dad hated flowers because he thought they were a waste of money, although he liked them in gardens, so we decided to set up a JustGiving site so people could donate the money they would have spent on flowers to charity. We decided on three charities: Marie Curie Cancer Care, St Luke's Hospice and the Samantha Dickson Brain Tumour Trust. Within seven minutes of it going live, there were ten donations.

We met with the funeral director and talked about what we wanted. We decided to have the funeral at the church where Mum and Dad had got married nineteen years before and we started to think about what music we should have and dig out photos of him. It was really difficult; Dad had never talked about what he wanted, he never thought he was going to die. Right up until the last breath I know he thought he would beat it, as we all did. We decided to cremate him.

The whole experience was completely surreal. I kept expecting him to walk through the front door and make a joke. Because it was a Bank Holiday weekend the hospital bed was still sat in the front room with all his sheets on and every time I walked in there it served as a painful reminder. I kept thinking about how his hugs felt, the exact pressure of his thick arms around me, exactly the way he spoke. I cannot believe that as I get older, his picture will stay young. My brain didn't stop whirring with thoughts about how unbelievable it felt.

On the Monday we went to see him at the Chapel of Rest. It was William's fifteenth birthday and Will was so gutted he had made it through mine and Ben's birthdays but not quite to his. He was lying in a coffin with his hands on his stomach and I hated the thought he would be like that when the lid was shut. He was cold and they had put make-up on him so he didn't look too white. We decided to bury him in his 'Give Me Oil in My Lamp' T-shirt. We knew he would have hated being in a suit. The year before, my brothers and I had bought him a 'No. 1 Dad' cuddly bear so we put that in the coffin with him and all wrote birthday cards, Father's Day cards and anniversary cards, which were all coming up.

I went back to training on Tuesday as normal. I knew he would not want me to stop. In his last days, he would ask me every time I was by his bed why I wasn't at training, even if it was midnight.

We tried to continue as normal and I had my driving theory test that Tuesday, which I passed. In my haste, I dialled the number I always did: Dad's. As it rang out I realized what I had done, hung up and rang Mum instead. Dad would always be the first person I spoke to.

The family really rallied around and everyone came over at least once a day. On one day Brooke and Malia were at home with us. I've always loved being with my young cousins.

'Where's Robert?' Brooke asked.

'He's gone out for a minute, Brookie,' I told her.

Later, up in my bedroom, I was with Malia and she asked so many lovely questions.

'Has Robert gone with the angels now?' she asked.

'Yes, he's an angel now,' I said.

'What – a man can be an angel?'

'Yes.'

'So where did he get dressed before he went to be an angel?'

'They get dressed automatically – it's like magic.'

'So if he's an angel, he can see me now?'

'Yes, he can,' I told her and she started waving out my bedroom window.

'Hi, Uncle Robert.'

'Every time I have a Creme Egg now, I'm going to think of Uncle Robert.'

Dad had used to joke with Malia that there was a special bird
that lays Cadbury's Creme Eggs and he had this special box he
decorated with glitter and each time she came round he would give
her the box and she would open it and there would be an egg inside
from the 'special' bird.

I was nervous about the funeral but knew I could never prepare
myself. About 500 people packed out the small church. I was just
going to go up to the rostrum and speak; I didn't prepare anything,
but the Vicar told me to jot a few words down in case my mind went
blank, so I did. We played 'Unchained Melody', which was the song
that Mum and Dad had their first dance to at their wedding, and the
congregation sang ' Sing Hosannah' because the words 'Give Me Oil
in My Lamp' had become so symbolic in Dad's battle.

When I stood up to speak I didn't use my sheet of notes, I just spoke
about the things that I remembered and will always remember
about Dad.

As I walked to the rostrum, I took my time. I had a horrible lump in my
throat and didn't want to cry. I talked about the normal stuff: how he
always used to make pancakes for us for breakfast, how he would
always take me to training and watch me, William and Ben do our
sports, how he'd always put on a brave face, how he was the practical
joker and all the memories everyone has of him. How whenever anyone
thinks of Rob Daley, they smile.

In the crematorium, it was a small private family ceremony. We played
Adele's 'Make You Feel My Love' as Dad was on the table. I could not
believe that was it.

Afterwards we all went to the wake at a nearby hotel and tried to remember the good times and drink in celebration of his life. Everyone who was there stopped me to say sorry, but I found it difficult to know what to say in response. There were pictures and videos of Dad on loop on the big screen.

That same day I had to go the National Championships in Leeds. I just needed to go because I knew Dad would have wanted me to go and perform as normal. I just wanted to do my best.

Pete and I were pulled out of the synchro that Friday because we had not had time to prepare.

I didn't get hung up on my performance. I just chatted to everyone as normal and tried to be how I always am. Of course I was sad and shocked and a million other emotions, but so much of my life involves compartmentalizing what is going on, so I just tried to focus on my diving and not think about Dad. I have been working like that for such a long time I do not find it an impossible task. Mum was there supporting me with all the other diving parents.

I didn't do any media because I was worried about getting upset, so I just released a statement saying: 'I came here because my Dad would have wanted me to be here. I have my main event in the 10m individual and I can't wait.'

In the 3m springboard I didn't do particularly well, finishing fifth overall, with victory going to Jack Laugher. In the individual, I was on fire in the prelims and was leading halfway through the final but eventually had to settle for second place in the final after not getting enough rotation speed on my front four and a half somersaults, which

cost me crucial points. I finished on 465.90 to Pete's 525.35 and Max was just 0.9 points behind me. Pete had struggled with his front four and a half, too, in the prelims after getting a failed dive because he only managed three and a half rotations. However, he executed it brilliantly in the final and earned three perfect 10s and a score of 107.30. The key is the start – it needs to be absolutely perfect. If you do not get enough height and speed, then it all goes to pot towards the latter end of the dive. Of course I was disappointed with my score, but I knew my preparation in the run-up to the competition wasn't great, and as my career progresses I find it hard to get into the same mental space as when I am at an international event with the atmosphere and pressure that brings.

After the National Championships it was Mum and Dad's anniversary, Dad's birthday and then Father's Day within a week. We went out for meals where we thought Dad would have liked to have gone. Father's Day was particularly hard because there were so many adverts everywhere. I know it's something I will have to get used to but it was weird. I was still so shocked and it just didn't seem real. I hope it gets easier.

In terms of my diving it was important to get back to training consistently and get into preparation mode prior to the Worlds. I was also revising for my AS levels as I had a Maths one, which didn't go very well.

I feel really responsible now towards my mum and I want to look after everyone. I feel it's my job to make sure we have enough money and I have to keep diving for that. I bought Mum a special Pandora bead to remind her of Dad. When we went on holiday to Spain once, we went to this Chinese restaurant and we joked that the Buddha was Dad, so I bought a special Buddha. Mum is so strong; she is amazing.

LOOKING TO 2012

Sooner or later, I knew, I would be back in the media spotlight and about three weeks after the funeral I travelled to London for a day of interviews around Get Set Go Free for Nestlé. I tried to put on a positive front and stuck to the same line – that Dad would want me to continue with my diving. I did some climbing on a wall at Potter's Fields in London to try and promote their latest campaign to get families into sport and, after a 5 a.m. start, did interviews with *Daybreak*, Sky, and various radio stations and newspapers.

I also did an interview with the *ES Magazine* for the *Evening Standard*, with some pictures of me diving in my uniform. The day before, some of the lines had been pulled out of the interview for the paper and on the front cover was 'Tom Daley's suicide threat revealed'. They had spoken to Andy and run with the line of me being homesick when I was younger, saying 'I would rather be dead' than be away.

EVERYONE AROUND ME WAS A BIT ANNOYED WITH THE WAY THEY HAD SPUN THE LINE UP BUT I DIDN'T CARE; I THOUGHT IT WAS QUITE AMUSING BECAUSE IT WAS SO FAR FROM THE TRUTH.

Then it was on to China. I didn't know whether I would be called 'Baby Daley' this time round – as I guess at 5ft 9in I would be about two foot taller than everyone there!

I was worried about leaving my mum and brothers at home but Mum's parents were going to stay, which made me feel a bit better, and I rang her every day.

First off we went to Xian for a two-week training camp. It was great to be back and we stayed in the Shangri-La again, which was amazing.

They had a ping-pong room there where we played this game called Ultimate Pong, which was basically like table tennis without the table. It was great to see all the other divers from around the world. We also went to see the Terracotta Army, which was pretty impressive.

From there we travelled to Shanghai. It was so humid; it felt like being in a giant steam room all the time. My popularity in China is bonkers. I am one of the most famous non-Chinese Olympians. I have nearly 1,000,000 followers on my Tencent Wiebo account – their equivalent of Twitter. On one day I was interviewed by all the Chinese newspapers and met sixteen fans who had flown in from cities across the country and everyone kept asking me if I have a girlfriend.

The outdoor pool was stunning and had a massive covered area for the spectators against a backdrop of the city's harbour. It felt like an indoor pool because it was so new and shiny. It rained a lot during training, which felt a bit strange, but there were also some sunny periods so I could top up my tan!

Almost as soon as we arrived, Pete got flu-like symptoms and we were almost going to pull out, deciding the day before the competition that we would compete.

Pete could not hear in one ear and it was fairly windy at the stadium. We started well with our inward one and a half somersaults but weren't able to maintain it after the Chinese managed five perfect 10s on their second round. We finished sixth with 407.56 points but we felt it was OK considering our preparation had not been very good. Huo Liang and Qiu picked up gold with 480.03, ahead of Germany on 443.01 and Ukraine on 435.36. We were happy that we had qualified the UK for a spot in the Olympics, but in some ways it felt like a missed opportunity.

UP THE GREAT WALL
OF CHINA. IT WAS
MUCH COLDER THAN
IT LOOKS!

THE TEAM DOING
OUR FAVOURITE
HANDSTAND
TRICK – NOT SURE
WHAT THE OTHER
TOURISTS WERE
THINKING!

On our last day in Xian we did a practice run-through, getting up at the time we would for the event, eating the same food, doing the same warm-up and waiting the same amount of time between dives. And for that we scored a personal best, so it was a little bit disappointing.

In the individual event I never expected to keep my title of World Champion. Qiu was unstoppable in the semi-finals, registering a set of perfect scores. The finals were delayed after a scary thunderstorm and when we finally did dive it was raining and there were some thunderclaps, which added to the drama! In the end Qiu won gold with 585.45 points, David Boudia got silver with 544.25, while Sascha Klein scored 534.50 for bronze. I beat the 90-point mark on two of my dives – my armstand back triple and my reverse three and a half – and while the rest of my list was steady, I ended fifth with 505.10. Although I would have loved to be on the podium, I still felt positive about my performance and knew that if I had performed all my dives to my best, I could have been there. Pete and I qualified the UK for two spots in the Olympics. And while Qiu is clearly consistent, there are at least eight other divers out there who can match his performance.

I know there is going to be a lot of expectation for London 2012. But people who know sport know that it doesn't just happen and it's not a totally foregone conclusion that I'm going to win gold in 2012. No way is that the case.

ANY OF THE TOP DIVERS IN THE WORLD COULD WIN THE GOLD MEDAL IF THEY DIVE WELL ON THE DAY. IT'S JUST ABOUT WHO HAS GOT THE RIGHT MENTALITY.

After the event it was a case of heading straight to London for the 'one year to go' celebrations. The London Aquatics Centre looked

incredible. There are three pools: one each for training, competition and diving. All three have floating floors so the depth can be adjusted, and there is no smell of chlorine as high-tech filters clean the water and cut down the need for chemicals. Watching my dive – the first ever at the stadium – there were only 1,500 people in a 17,500-person auditorium, but the noise was deafening. It was incredible.

I was really nervous as normally I have a long warm-up to get psyched up, so I decided to do one of my easier dives, my one and a half piked, which I do in synchro. I was worried that if I did one of my more complicated dives and it went wrong I might look like a tit! I was also considering doing a crazy dive bomb – I wonder what everyone would have done.

They wanted me to walk slowly up the stairs to build up as much drama as possible. As I reached the end of the board, I thought, 'This is just a small taste of what it is going to be like next year.' The same deafening cheers, rush of adrenalin and overwhelming excitement. I felt more motivated and focused than ever.

Then the countdown began. The noise was ear-popping.

Ten, nine, eight, seven, six, five, four, three, two, one.

I was laughing as I flew through the air.

IT WAS A PERFECT DIVE.

EPILOGUE

On New Year's Eve, I was out in Looe. For one night a year this sleepy Cornish town comes alive with fireworks and street parties as friends and families get dressed up in fancy dress to see in the New Year together by the seafront.

I was with my cousin Sam, Sophie and Nikita and we went dressed as 2012. As a group we are closer than ever and barely a days goes past when we don't all hang out together. We had picked up Sophie from work at about six o'clock in my car – I passed my driving test in September – and we had driven down to the caravan site where we were spending the night and had taken ages getting our costumes ready.

We were each wearing one of the numbers – Sophie was '2', I was 'O', Nikita was '1' and Sam was the other '2'. We cut the shapes of the numbers from old furniture boxes and spray-painted them gold, then edged them with gold tinsel. We also painted our faces yellow and put fairy lights around our heads. There was no missing us!

As we headed out at about 9 o'clock the streets were filled with people and there wasn't a single person who wasn't dressed up. Tonia was there – she went with a group of friends dressed as crayons. There were lots of Marios and people in tiger onesies. It was a brilliant atmosphere. People didn't recognize me from far away but when they got closer they did. I didn't even recognize myself!

Every time someone said '2012' we cheered and we had loads of laughs trying to stay in formation all the time and not lose the '2's. 'Number 2, get over here.' I kept bumping into friends from Plymouth College and everyone stopped to talk to each other. The others had a few drinks but I stuck to my Diet Coke and lemonade.

December had been a brilliant month. On the 1st, I flew to Australia for a three-week training camp with the GB team. Our Performance Director, Alexei took us there to get away from all the colds and flu in this country and to soak up some sunshine to build up our immune systems, which was ace! We were in Sydney for one week then went to Adelaide for two. We trained every day in the pool and the gym. I was working on keeping my dives as consistent and confident as possible and had quite a lot of time to relax and have fun on the beach. Outside of training I spent most of my time with Jack Laugher and Chris Mears. Pete wasn't with us because he wanted to stay with his two young kids in the run-up to Christmas.

I did a bit of homework while I was away – I knew that after my exams in January, my focus would solely be on the Games. I have always enjoyed studying but from January onwards I would be in the pool as much as possible. Then I would be off to competitions in London, Dubai, Russia, Mexico and Holland with training camps in Plymouth, Majorca and Southend before the Olympics.

We arrived back home on Christmas Eve and I was really looking forward to seeing everyone again. We had a normal Christmas Day at my Grandma Jenny's and then went to my Aunty Marie's on Boxing

Day. Of course I thought about Dad but we were too busy to spend ages moping and whenever we talk about him, it's always in a positive and proud way. I try never to dwell on the fact he was taken from us too early, just the good stuff; the advice he gave me and the values he instilled in me. In some ways I feel like he's still here, standing beside me. I know whatever I do and whatever I achieve in the future, he would be the proudest man on earth.

As the countdown started and the clock struck midnight, we were on the beach. A huge cheer went up, the fireworks started, and we had a big group hug. My heart started beating really fast as it hit me that the Olympics were this year. They were no longer next year, it was this year and I knew that would change the way I both thought and spoke about it. I felt like the time had gone so quickly, it was unreal.

I called my mum who was with Ben at her cousin Rachel's house. I didn't think I'd get through but I did and it felt brilliant to be able to wish her a happy New Year. My family didn't make a big point of it being Olympics year as they don't want to heap any unnecessary pressure on me, but I feel so excited and happy. I know I'll have the advantage of all the support and feel like despite being four years older than I was when we went to Beijing in 2008, I know I've got more Olympics ahead of me. I'd love to compete in five and keep diving professionally until I am 30.

As a team we have loads of confidence. I can't wait to savour every second of the Olympic experience: being in the village, watching the other athletes, the immense rush of adrenalin and hopefully, performing the best dives of my life.

Nothing has changed since I was eight years old and drew that picture of myself. I'm a perfectionist and I'm going for gold.

THANKS TO:

My family for supporting me from the very beginning and making me feel like whatever I did, it was always great!

My friends, you are the ones that are always there and you never seem to stop making me laugh!

My fans, you are awesome! And I can't wait to see you all in London for the Olympic Games very soon :)

My agents at Professional Sports Group: Michela Chiappa, Charlotte Hallam and Jamie Cunningham for organising my life and helping everything move forward.

Georgina Rodgers, who helped me tell me story, and thanks also to Jonathan Harris.

My editor Dan Bunyard for bringing the book to life and to Andrew Smith for designing it.

My coach Andy for keeping me in the pool and guiding me to the diver I have become today.

My dad Rob, who I will always love and never forget.

PICTURE CREDITS:

Page 1 Image courtesy of adidas © Clive Rose/ Getty Images, post-production by Michel Groot; Pages 2-3, 12-13, 26-7, 30-1, 43, 62-3, 94-5, 96-7, 98, 101, 108, 147, 206-7, 222, 231, 244, 271 © Andy Hooper; Pages 5-6, 8-9, 38, 83 © Andy Hooper/*Daily Mail*/Solo Syndication; Pages 6-7, 43 © Elise Dumontet; Pages 72-3, 187, 219, 229, 248-9, 284-5 © Jonathan Glynn-Smith; Pages 44-5, 116-17 © *Daily Mail*/Rex/Alamy; Pages 52-3, 80-1, 102, 106-7, 149, 156, 246 © Mirrorpix; Pages 56, 77 © Perou/Camera Press London; Page 65 © Martin Bureau/Getty Images; Pages 71, 84, 135, 158, 172-3 © Rex Features; Pages 74, 110-11, 132-3, 270 x 2 © Press Association Images; Pages 87, 136-7 © Karen Robinson/Camera Press London; Page 88 © Martin Pope/ Camera Press London; Pages 115, 275 © Ben Duffy; Page 120 © Leon Neal/Getty Images; Pages 122-3 © Simon Jessop/Camera Press London; Pages 125 x 2 © Daniel Berehulak/Getty Images; Pages 138-9 © Cameron Spencer/Getty Images; Pages 141 © David Rogers/Getty Images; Pages 142, 143 © Julian Finney/ Getty Images; 142 © Jeff Gross/Getty Images; Page 145 © Chen Kai/ Xinhua Press/Corbis; Pages 154-5 © Visionhaus/Corbis; Pages 178-9 © Marc Giddings/*The Sun*; Page 180 © Adrian Sherratt/Alamy; Pages 200-1 © Bruce Weber; Pages 208-9 © Guy Levy/ Comic Relief; Page 212 © Adam Pretty/Getty Images; Page 236 © Nick Wilkinson/ epa/Corbis; Page 238 © Clive Rose/Getty Images; Page 239 © Feng Li/Getty Images; Pages 252-3 © Dave Rowntree; Page 264 © Vaughn Ridley/SWpix.com; Pages 272-3 © Camera Press London; Pages 281, 282 © WPA Pool/Getty Images; Endpapers © Andy Hooper, Andy Hooper/*Daily Mail*/Solo Syndication, Andy Hooper/ Associated Newspapers/Rex Features, Mirrorpix, Jonathan Glynn-Smith, Rex Features, Ben Duffy, Simon Jessop/ Camera Press London, *Daily Mail*/Rex/Alamy, Jeff Gross/ Getty Images, Adam Pretty/Getty Images, Martin Bureau/ Getty Images, WPA Pool/Getty Images, Chen Kai/Xinhua Press/Corbis, Guy Levy/Comic Relief, Dave Rowntree, Elise Dumontet.

Every effort has been made to trace copyright holders. The publishers will be glad to rectify in future editions any errors or omissions brought to their attention.